ADVANCE PRAISE

"Brilliant! Required reading for any lawyer looking to take their firm to the next level."

—BRIAN LIU, FOUNDER AND CEO OF LEGALZOOM
AND BIZCOUNSEL AND LEADER IN LEGAL TECH

"Reza Torkzadeh has written a terrific book about how to manage a law firm for growth and success. Indeed, the many insights in this book will be of great value to any business or organization. The book is both practical in its recommendations and inspirational in showing what can be achieved."

—ERWIN CHEMERINSKY, DEAN, AND JESSE H. CHOPER
DISTINGUISHED PROFESSOR OF LAW, UNIVERSITY
OF CALIFORNIA, BERKELEY SCHOOL OF LAW

"Reza outlines the simple but important management principles he used to build a highly successful practice through this quick read."

—HON. PETER POLOS, RETIRED SUPERIOR COURT JUDGE

"*I have watched Reza Torkzadeh grow his firm into a nationally recognized and respected law firm using technology, culture, and executing on his vision. He not only shares his story but gives the reader a step-by-step path on how to do it. A must-read!*"

—HARLAN SCHILLINGER, LEGAL MARKETING EXPERT
WITH OVER FOUR DECADES OF EXPERIENCE IN
LEGAL MARKETING, INTAKE, AND CONVERSION

"*The Lawyer as CEO should be required reading for lawyers in all practice areas, regardless of how many years they've been in practice. It is a practical blueprint for readers to focus their law firm on technology and culture in order to successfully execute their vision as CEO.*"

—ANTHONY JOHNSON, FOUNDER OF JOHNSON FIRM,
LEADING PLAINTIFF'S ATTORNEY, AND WIDELY KNOWN
AS ONE OF AMERICA'S "TECHIEST" LAWYERS

"*A thoughtfully and candidly written strategy for a successful law firm from the head of one of the nation's most progressive firms. A must-read for every CEO, senior partner, and managing partner of all law firms.*"

—ALLEN WILKINSON, ESQ. LEGAL SCHOLAR,
AUTHOR, AND RESEARCHER

"*Reza lays out a roadmap to transform and modernize your firm's organization. Every law school should teach these lessons. This book should be required reading for anyone looking for growth— both personally and professionally.*"

—MIKE ALDER, ESQ. FOUNDER OF ALDERLAW

"*Reza brilliantly lays out the argument for culture and running your firm as a Fortune 500 company in The Lawyer as CEO.*"

—BRIAN PANISH, ESQ. FOUNDER OF PANISH
SHEA BOYLE RAVIPUDI, LLP

THE LAWYER AS CEO

REZA TORKZADEH

THE LAWYER AS CEO

Stay Competitive, Attract Better Talent,
and Get Your Clients Results
(While Building the Law Firm of the Future)

LIONCREST
PUBLISHING

THE LAWYER AS CEO
Stay Competitive, Attract Better Talent, and Get Your Clients Results (While Building the Law Firm of the Future)

FIRST EDITION

ISBN   978-1-5445-3113-7 *Hardcover*
       978-1-5445-3114-4 *Paperback*
       978-1-5445-3115-1 *Ebook*

To my beautiful wife, who has given me the three greatest gifts of my life: my two daughters and the unconditional love and support of me and my dreams, no matter how crazy they are.

CONTENTS

One hundred percent of all proceeds from the sale of this book will be donated to the Los Angeles Trial Lawyers' Charities (LATLC) and Orange County Trial Lawyers' Charities (OCTLC).

FOREWORD

—MICHAEL MOGILL, FOUNDER AND CEO OF CRISP, BEST-SELLING AUTHOR, AND HOST OF *THE GAME CHANGING ATTORNEY* PODCAST

My first thought when I finished this book was *Reza is right*.

The legal industry has changed. Gone are the days when you could have a successful practice simply by being a great lawyer. Your law firm now has to face increased competition, mega-firm consolidation, and a future in which outside players with limitless resources are free to enter your market and make your life miserable.

This isn't hyperbole or some distant future. In fact, I've seen this dynamic play out time and time again at Crisp, the company I founded. We're the largest law firm coaching company in the nation, and we support nearly a thousand law firm owners in every practice area across the country: big and small, urban and rural, young and old. From that unique vantage point, I can see that the single biggest indicator of success for a law firm in this rapidly evolving legal landscape is the mindset of the firm owner. Specifically, do they approach their law firm as a business?

As Reza lays out in these pages, to compete in this new world, you can't *just* be a great attorney anymore. You have to be a great CEO.

While "business" may sound like a dirty word to some, Reza capably relates how introducing a business mindset into your firm is not only key to its survival—it's also the blueprint to providing better service. By implementing Reza's ideas, you can prioritize and improve your client experience, bring in the best talent, create a positive and resilient firm culture, and implement technology to give yourself an edge in a market that usually favors the biggest advertisers over the best lawyers.

The people who benefit the most from this shift will be the ones who depend on you the most: your clients, your team, and your community.

If you believe in helping people, changing lives, and making a positive impact on those around you, you have a duty to follow Reza's advice and become the leader your firm needs. That's how you'll keep your doors open and your firm thriving.

Luckily, in this book, you'll be learning how to accomplish this transition from someone who leads by example. Reza has built one of the fastest growing law firms in the country. What he's managed to accomplish in one of the nation's most competitive markets is inspiring. And in this book, he lays out his best ideas as well as many of his early missteps.

For those of you who have yet to evolve your firm, time is running out. Remaining competitive is already difficult, and it's about to get a lot more challenging. You don't have the luxury of ignoring the importance of business management that the last generation of lawyers did. You have to decide right now whether you're going to build your law firm of the future or lose out to someone else who did.

The choice is yours, but if you want to build a firm that can withstand whatever the future holds, the answers are ahead.

INTRODUCTION

I'm going to predict the future for you.

Within the next ten years, the chances your firm can succeed in the legal field will go from unlikely to impossible. Venture capitalists and other stakeholders will get the laws changed in almost every state and then swoop in and buy every firm they can get their hands on. Once they've consolidated their new megafirms, they'll institute policies to maximize profitability. There will be no heart, no personality, and no individuality in these firms—but there will be immense success. They will be ruthless profit machines that use their massive budgets to flood the market with advertising, buy up the best legal talent, and starve the competition. They'll bring in top CEOs straight off Wall Street, use the latest technology and business practices, and run their firms like hyper-aggressive Fortune 500 companies.

Some of these firms may even become Fortune 500 companies.

In the meantime, firms like yours will shrivel up and die. It won't matter how much you care about your clients or justice or your community. It won't matter how good a lawyer you are. It will simply become impossible to survive, let alone scale as you once had hoped.

Without the financial resources or the know-how of the private-equity-backed megafirms, your firm and the vast majority of up-and-coming firms across the country will become obsolete. They'll go the way of Altavista, Ask Jeeves, and Yahoo once Google overwhelmed the search engine industry.

This prediction sounds like a nightmare, but unfortunately, it isn't some crazy, fevered nightmare of the future. I didn't need to read any tea leaves or consult any oracles to come up with this vision. This transition is happening right now. Laws have already been passed in Arizona to allow non-lawyers to own and run firms. The California Bar is considering similar ideas right now—potentially allowing non-lawyers to practice law! That's the first step to investor-funded Wall Street CEOs leading law firms.

As things stand, the end seems nigh. But there is hope. The lawyer-run individual firm can still lead our industry—but only if we start building firms fit for this future today.

LAW FIRMS HAVE TO CHANGE NOW

Here's the good news. Though this future may be inevitable, the more traditional law firm can still succeed and thrive—by any measure against any competition. The way we outcompete these future megafirms is by taking the best ideas from Wall Street companies and investors and incorporating those ideas into the current structure of our firms. If we start on this project now, we can build efficient firms that care about clients, provide quality work opportunities, develop sterling reputations, and achieve fantastic levels of scale before the megafirms ever get up and running. And we can do all of this without the cut-throat, profit-at-all-costs venture capitalists coming in and taking over our law businesses.

We can only take this step, though, if we recognize how far we are from the standards set by most businesses. Right now, there are investors standing in statehouses claiming—accurately— that law firms don't provide the same level of service or access to their clients that customers get in almost every other field. Compared to grocery stores, restaurants, car repair shops, and doctors' offices, law firms have fallen far behind service expectations. Likewise, law firms don't offer nearly the consistent quality office experience found in other industries. Firms lack company culture, consistent motivation, and innovation that are standard in other types of business.

Within this limitation, though, there is an opportunity. By simply investing in the same strategies other industries have already integrated, we can grow at a fantastic pace. These ideas have become the standard in other industries because they work. Running your firm like a Fortune 500 company does produce results. It can allow your firm to compete today with the most dominant firms in your city—and perhaps even scale beyond them.

The big-money investors aren't wrong. The law industry does need a shakeup. What I'm asking you to do is shake it up yourself and show the results.

TWO LAW FIRMS, ONE PROBLEM

This is easier said than done, of course. For many lawyers, the possibility of scaling their firm seems an impossible task. Most likely, that's because you're likely running one of the two main types of struggling law practices: a "False Start" firm or a "Stalled" firm.

False Start law firms just can't seem to get much purchase in the legal market. They are usually manned by a single lawyer (or a couple partners) and, at most, one or two administrative assistants. There's a trickle of clients, but for some reason, it never increases beyond a trickle. After a few years, it's clear that there hasn't been much progress, and it's hard to see where progress is going to come from.

Is this your firm?

Maybe not. Maybe yours is a Stalled firm. These are firms that have got some purchase in the market, but just a bit. They may have enough incoming clients to afford another lawyer or two and a small staff to accommodate the workflow; however, once these firms reach a certain size, they stop growing. They get just big enough to know that growth is possible, but before they can get on the highway and accelerate toward a more impressive scale, they stall.

After some early promise as a False Start or Stalled firm, you may assume that your law practice isn't likely to mount much competition against the megafirms. But that doesn't have to be the case, and the solution is far more straightforward than you might imagine.

A common problem at False Start and Stalled firms is that the lawyer at the top simply lacks the ideas and strategies used by successful CEOs. The lack of growth has little to do with investment or legal experience, as most lawyers assume, but is instead the result of poor organizational development—a failure to prioritize customer service, smart technology, company culture, and authentic, modern marketing techniques.

All of this can be corrected if you are equipped to take on the role of CEO and focus your attention on these priorities. You can be one of the examples that prove how effectively lawyers can manage their own business. And this book will show you how.

Attorneys who come to my firm, TorkLaw, or my legal networking group, LawWorks, all say the same thing: "I want my firm to be at the top of the industry." They say it in such a wishful way, as if they don't believe such a thing is possible. But it is. And what's more, it doesn't require a massive investment or a brilliant marketing strategist. It certainly doesn't require the input of venture capitalists.

Instead, success at the highest level of the legal field comes down to whether that lawyer standing in my office is willing to look at their firm as a business and build it around basic business fundamentals.

That's the secret. That's all it takes.

STOP THINKING LIKE A LAWYER

How effective is this new way of leading your law firm?

It can beat a pandemic.

For most firms, 2020 was the year of COVID, shutdowns, and economic devastation. For TorkLaw, it was our best year ever. The world came to a stop, the courts were closed, no one could go to the office—and we were bringing in clients at record numbers.

That success was possible because, years before, I'd changed how I thought about running a law firm. I stopped running it like other firms and started running it like the most successful corporations on the planet. I took the best strategies implemented across various industries and introduced them to TorkLaw.

The insight to do this came out of a moment of frustration. I found myself unhappy and frustrated at my own firm. In 2012, I'd left a relatively prosperous practice I'd started with partners and went out on my own. Just after saying "I do" to my wife, I'd told her I needed to build a new firm, one that spoke my beliefs and ambitions.

I wanted to have a firm with a reach across the country, a firm that could help thousands of personal injury clients a year. I wanted to build a massive, national firm with its heart in the right place.

I was ready to focus, take risks, and put everything into achieving that dream. I was so prepared, in fact, I was willing to start the firm in a spare bedroom in the condo we'd just purchased (one that we couldn't really afford now that I was leaving my old partnership). To get up and running, I charged expenses on credit cards and borrowed money from family and friends.

In those early months, I did everything: I was the firm's receptionist, its paralegal, its marketing department, and its trial lawyer. That early effort paid off. Over a couple years, the firm grew enough that I was able to hire a small team of lawyers, paralegals, and administrators. I thought I was on my way.

Yet as the firm grew, somehow things got worse. The office developed an extremely toxic culture. Growth slowed. I had high turnover and unhappy clients. Eventually, the situation got so bad, I hated going into the office. I had no idea what I was doing wrong. I felt stuck—*stalled* even.

Hard as it may be to believe, I was able to turn that situation around and build a firm that is now in eight states and twelve cities—and growing, even in a pandemic.

Once I went from the passive lawyer who focused on his cases to the CEO in complete control of the firm, I was able to make the critical changes at the core of the firm that would allow it to adapt and grow. I built a culture centered on my beliefs in justice and how to treat people. I instituted expansive customer-friendly policies and processes. I made sure to invest in any technology that could improve those priorities.

I didn't invent the tools that allowed my firm to weather once-in-a-century pandemics and to scale at a blinding rate. All I did was borrow from the business principles you'll find in every Wall Street playbook.

When those players make moves to take over the law industry, my firm won't be a sitting duck because I've already learned to build a highly successful law practice that can compete on its own.

Now it's your turn to do the same.

A BLOCKBUSTER MOMENT

As lawyers, we can learn so much from business. For instance, let me tell you a story about a little video rental company you might have heard of: Blockbuster. In the early 2000s, Blockbuster was at the top of their industry. There were thousands of Blockbuster stores across the country, and the number seemed to grow by the hour. A well-developed business model for rentals had led them to the pinnacle of business success.

While Blockbuster stores kept multiplying, the company had opportunities to buy two separate companies: Netflix and Redbox. In fact, Netflix actually approached Blockbuster to purchase their company back in 2000. Blockbuster chose to go its own way and stick with what was already working.

We all know the rest of the story. Every home in the country has a Netflix account, and every supermarket has a Redbox. Blockbuster has faded so much from the collective memory that parents had to explain the reference to their children during the *Captain Marvel* movie. From over nine thousand stores at its height, today, only one Blockbuster store remains—in Bend, Oregon.

Law firms are now facing our own Blockbuster moment. Up

until now, certain strategies have allowed for success. Some of those traditional strategies may even be working for you right now. However, like Blockbuster, whether we want to recognize it or not, our industry has stopped scaling the mountain and instead stands upon the cliff's edge. If we want to compete, we have to avoid Blockbuster's mistake and open our doors to innovation and new ideas.

Imagine if Blockbuster had leveraged all of its customer data and launched a Blockbuster-Netflix hybrid with Blockbuster-Redboxes at every store. We'd be talking about one of the most successful companies in the world right now, not the stuff of '90s nostalgia.

If law firms meet this moment, we are primed for great success. While private equity may bring with it untold stock market riches, we, like Blockbuster, know this industry in a way they simply can't. We know the law, the needs of our clients, the legal process, and our communities intimately. *We* have the unfair advantage—not them—and *we* can maximize that. But only if we accept the changes coming and adapt early enough.

That's the choice we face as law firms today: the potential to reach new heights or the potential to become irrelevant as the paradigm shifts.

THIS COULD BE YOU...IF YOU CARE ENOUGH

I had lunch with an old friend the other day, a lawyer who founded his own firm around the time I started TorkLaw. We were out enjoying the spring weather and the chance to actually sit across from one another now that the pandemic is beginning to wind down. As we settled in and began to catch up, the subject of success came up.

"We started at the same time and in the same place," my friend said. "How is it that your firm has grown so much faster?"

I considered the question a moment. "In part, I got lucky!" I conceded. "I landed some good cases at the right time. And some of it was sheer grit. I refused to let anyone outwork me, even in all the years it took to get my firm off the ground."

Yet that wasn't the sum of the difference. Grit and luck play their part in any success story, but the difference between my firm and my friend's is how much I cared to reach for the top. My friend is a great person, and he likes the law, but he's happy running a small firm. I wouldn't recommend this book to him.

There's nothing wrong with running a firm like my friend's. There's nothing wrong with small if that's what you want. He takes on a few clients, and he's happy to work on those terms. This book wouldn't work for him because he doesn't *care* about scaling his firm. He doesn't need to be a CEO because he's happy simply being a lawyer and keeping things small.

And I hope he can somehow keep that going when the market changes.

If you want more than that—and if you want to ensure success no matter how big the competition gets—scale isn't out of reach. Becoming a lawyer-CEO isn't some special ability I brought to my firm. Any lawyer can do it—so long as they *care* enough to maximize their firm's potential. If you truly care about serving your clients, taking care of your community, developing an elite office, and reaching the top of the profession, the ideas in this book will help you achieve that.

With this book, you can harness the motivations that drive you to be a great lawyer and create a firm that can grow in any future. That's what is within your grasp if you care enough to read on and prove that you're CEO material.

PART I

IT STARTS WITH YOU

CHAPTER 1

A SMALL FIRM IN A BIG WORLD

Whether they have a False Start or Stalled law firm, there's one universal feeling that unites all struggling lawyers: the sense that someone has already snatched up most of the pie. No matter the city or the area of law, everyone believes the big firms competing in their space have an unfair advantage. They had the chance to get started earlier, get established, and now they've taken far more than their fair share of the business. And there's no way to change that dynamic.

Or so the thinking goes.

It's not hard to see why many lawyers trying to build firms feel this way. Driving along the highway and looking at those massive billboards while the radio plays ad after ad from these established, large firms, it does seem like there's no room left for a competitor. The big firms are on TV. They're at the top of every Google search. They're on the sides of busses. They sponsor professional sports teams and marathons.

That's a lot of expensive advertising, and there's no way a smaller firm can keep up—certainly not on a dollar-for-dollar investment.

What's worse, this advertising advantage seems to work. Ask a random person on the street to name a law firm, and they'll almost certainly name one of the big firms with massive advertising budgets in your city. It's only natural. It's the name they see and hear almost every day of their lives.

The solution seems obvious: put all your resources into buying billboards, tv and radio ads, and wait for the clients to come flooding in. Unfortunately, this strategy is often the quickest route to failure.

Every few months, on the way to work, I'll see a new billboard with the name of a lawyer I've never heard of before. They always look confident, serious, and ready to serve, with a catchy slogan and the number to their office in big bold lettering at the bottom. If you didn't know better, you'd assume this was an advertisement straight out of the marketing department at one of Los Angeles's most successful firms.

But it doesn't come from one of those firms. And, inevitably, it's never long before that ad comes down and I find out that firm has gone out of business.

So are you meant to simply accept your place in the market and wait for the megafirms to come and eat up what little business you have? Is a Stalled or False Start firm all you can hope for? Not at all. But if you actually want to compete in this industry, you have to stop doing what the big firms already do and find a better way to build a business.

STOP TRYING TO KEEP UP WITH JONES, JONES, AND JONES

Let me say at the outset that all advertising works. Billboards do bring in clients. TV, radio, print, digital, social, pay-per-click. It all works. That's why big firms invest in them. However, not all advertising works for every firm. If you have a massive advertising budget, you can afford big outlays on sponsorships and TV ads. If you don't have that budget, trying to compete on that level is only going to lead to trouble.

I know this is not what you want to hear. When searching for a solution to any problem, we have a natural desire to copy what seems to work. I'm sure you remember the kids in school who would look around in desperation during a test and try to get a peek at what the best student in class was writing on the essay. Maybe you were the ace student or maybe you were the peeker. The dynamic is always the same, though.

That instinct is still with us. When we don't know what we're doing, we look to those who we assume do know and we imitate them. This is made all the easier by the fact that many lawyers start out at one of those bigger firms. They've seen how many clients come into the office because the firm name is on a billboard, radio, or tv commercial. They assume all they have to do is copy what they see in the big office and apply it to their smaller one.

After all, who knows better about running a successful firm than your big established competitors who are taking all the clients?

The answer to that question may not be as simple as you think it is. To begin with, just because a firm is big doesn't mean it is successfully run. It does not mean that they have a good office culture or satisfied clients who recommend them. Nor does all that advertising necessarily translate into the kind of client numbers or profit margins you'd expect when looking at them from the outside.

It's also worth keeping in mind that successful firms today are not guaranteed to be successful tomorrow. Take a look at the biggest companies from 1967. How many of those companies proved to be well-run enough to maintain their market dominance in the decades to come? Some, certainly, made smart choices, including AT&T, but others proved incapable of navigating a changing market. Sears barely exists anymore. Kodak and Polaroid have both tumbled into obscurity and bankruptcy. Anyone following those companies' lead would be setting themselves up for failure.

100 Years of America's Top 10 Companies ($B)

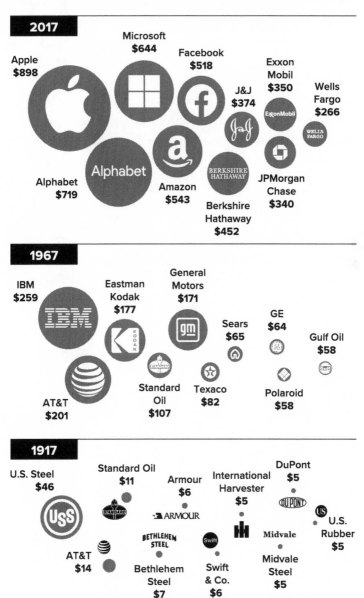

2017

Microsoft $644

Facebook $518

Apple $898

Exxon Mobil $350

Wells Fargo $266

J&J $374

Alphabet $719

Alphabet

Amazon $543

Berkshire Hathaway $452

JPMorgan Chase $340

1967

IBM $259

Eastman Kodak $177

General Motors $171

Sears $65

GE $64

Gulf Oil $58

AT&T $201

Standard Oil $107

Texaco $82

Polaroid $58

1917

U.S. Steel $46

Standard Oil $11

Armour $6

International Harvester $5

DuPont $5

U.S. Rubber $5

AT&T $14

Bethlehem Steel $7

Swift & Co. $6

Midvale Steel $5

Success in one particular moment can be an illusion, coming down to inertia after an initial period of innovation and excellent management. And law firms are no different. Most of the big firms of today have been big for a long time. Their success came in a previous era with different expectations and different rules. They can afford to maintain those old strategies because all they have to do is avoid slowing down. But keeping a big ship afloat is different than building a new boat. There's no reason to assume the lawyers managing those big firms could use the same strategies to scale a new firm in the modern, hyper-competitive market we have today.

So when lawyers with struggling firms simply copy the strategies they see from big firms—including everything from how to advertise to how to run an office and treat clients—they may very well be copying not from the best student in class, but one working from a textbook forty years out of date.

Even when these strategies aren't so outdated, what works on an enterprise level rarely scales down directly. This would be like trying to create a niche online search engine and advertiser to compete with Google by simply trying to copy what Google does as the preeminent industry leader and scale down to a small business size. You'd be dooming yourself to failure.

In fact, direct copying doesn't even work when you have the size and money to back the project. Microsoft proved this for us. They spent billions on developing a rival to Google called Bing. They even got caught lifting some of Google's search algorithm. Today, no one even uses their search engine. They have about 5 percent of the market while Google has held steady at 85 percent.

Microsoft was starting from a position of reasonable strength as a large, established tech company. Imagine if they'd tried to do this without their billions of dollars and teams of elite developers!

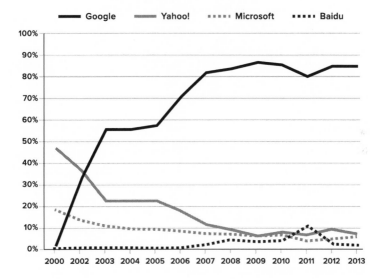

Global Search Market Share

The truth is, facing off against Google directly is business suicide. To compete with Google, you have to focus not on what Google does but what it doesn't do. That's why the tech company that has come to rival Google for digital dominance isn't a search engine but one that did something completely different: Facebook.

The same is true of your law firm. You won't match up against the big firms by trying to directly implement their business strategies in your much smaller office. If you want to compete, you'll need to develop your own strategies.

PUT THE EGO ASIDE

What do you do about that name recognition, then? How do you compete against the firms that are on billboards on the side of every highway that every driver stares at every day on the way to work?

First, you have to realize that size and reach isn't the advantage you think it is. While you know everything about those big firms—their history, reputation, and record—that isn't the experience of the average person.

Your assumption that a big firm is infinitely better known than yours comes down to a psychological phenomenon called Baader–Meinhof, or frequency illusion, that we all experience from time to time. Think about the last time you bought a car and started driving it down the highway. Suddenly, you saw that many of your fellow drivers had bought the same make and model as you. This isn't because you were some kind of massive vehicular trendsetter. Your mind was simply focused on the type of car you bought and you noticed what normally passed you by.

This is how the law industry is for most people. The average person hardly ever thinks about lawyers. Their only conscious thoughts about lawyers revolve around the TV shows they watch or the rare lawyer who makes the news. When they drive to work, they don't pay attention to those billboard ads. When the radio or TV ads come on, they change the channel. While they probably do know the name of one big firm or another if asked—and that does translate into some influx of clients when you are at a certain level of scale—that average person has no particular impression about that or any lawyer in their community. At least, not until they need one.

That means, despite the difference in advertising budgets, you have every opportunity to still compete for that client once they are actively looking for a lawyer. While you do need to get your name out there, extensive, expensive advertising isn't necessarily more successful at convincing that client to go to one firm over another.

So what is the point of those billboards or the big sponsorship deals?

If you're a big firm, it definitely gets some people in the door. But if you're smaller, it really only amounts to vanity. People like seeing their faces blown up on billboards. They like seeing their name on the sides of busses and hearing it on the radio. And they will spend far more than they need to—and deprioritize other needs in their firm—in order to make that a reality.

These expensive vanity projects are extremely tempting, as I've discovered myself. In 2021, TorkLaw was approached with just that kind of ego-stroking opportunity. A major professional sports team wanted us to be their official law firm. I very seriously considered the offer—until I thought about what our return would be. It sounded cool, but I knew that investment could go to other needs in the firm that would promote Tork-Law better at that moment. Essentially, I couldn't conceive of a way that sponsorship would translate to more clients than simply maximizing the strategies I already had in place. How many people who needed a personal injury lawyer would hear of me from that venue, who wouldn't have heard of me through the outreach we did elsewhere? Would that number actually justify the cost of the sponsorship?

Reviewing these hypotheticals, I quickly realized the strongest justification for the sponsorship was my ego. I liked the idea of my firm being this big, fancy official sponsor.

Vanity doesn't only manifest in advertising decisions. This lawyerly ego can lead to many miscalculations at Stalled or False Start firms, including hiring too much staff, buying up too much office space, or turning down small cases. Lawyers make these choices because, after growing frustrated at the slow pace of growth, they want to feel like they're already the big success they dream of becoming—with a big caseload handled by a big team of brilliant administrators all under a big billboard sign with their face on it. They start to think, "How can a *big* lawyer work with a modest team, in a small office, and take the 'scrap' cases the established firms turned down?"

You can imagine where this ego leads: to a lot of struggle with budget trouble on the horizon.

I'm not saying there's no room for ego in your work. Ego is a natural part of being a lawyer. It takes ego to get in front of a jury and argue a case. It takes ego to go out there and open a firm against all the odds. And ego may have helped keep you going when the firm hit a rough period.

This ego is deserved. You have an important and powerful position in our society. You can help people in a direct way that very few others can. And you do that work better when you have an intense sense of self-belief than if you give in to doubt and second-guessing.

However, it's important to recognize that ego-fueled ad buys, staff growth, and client selection won't build your firm. Trying to keep up with the big firms by pretending to be a big firm will only lead to trouble.

What will help you scale, though, is taking that ego and using it to *take control*. Recognize your role as a founder and business owner, and own this firm by leading it with innovation.

A billboard or a huge office space isn't going to lead to the client caseload you want. However, a well-run, highly motivated team that represents your values and hard work while serving well-satisfied clients can.

The trick to scaling your firm, then, isn't an ego buy or an ego investment; it's embracing your role as a leader and using the right business strategies to forge a new kind of law firm success.

GETTING BACK TO (BUSINESS) BASICS

I don't blame lawyers for chasing bad business strategies. After all, they don't teach business in law school. In fact, they leave you with the assumption that the key to success in this field comes down to being a good lawyer. It's doing the research, developing the legal strategies, negotiating hard, and winning your cases. The rest, it's implied, will take care of itself.

Being a good lawyer is extremely important. I don't want to take anything away from that. However, just as most people don't really notice those billboards, they also don't really know how to tell the difference between a good lawyer and a bad one. Every legal site says they've won big cases and claim they are the best in the business. Your clients have no idea whether you actually are as good as you claim or if you are just another lawyer making a big claim out of nothing.

In the eyes of your clients, then, you're no different than every other lawyer—no matter your legal skill. The difference makers in this industry are the same as in any other:

- How well does your staff perform their jobs?
- How well do they take care of your clients?
- How do your clients—and your staff—know you really care?
- What are you doing to make everyone's life easier?

None of that comes through when you talk about legal skills or winning cases. Instead, it requires getting back to the basic rules of running a business, the most basic of which is that you need a CEO in place to answer all these questions and implement those answers.

The buck has to stop with that CEO. And at your law firm, that CEO has to be you.

CHAPTER 2

BECOMING A CEO

I thought I had the whole law firm thing figured out. TorkLaw was growing—maybe not as much as I would have liked, but still growing. We were financially successful—not as successful as my ambitions had hoped, but still successful. We were adding clients, adding employees, and getting more office space.

I should have been happy. I'd transformed a one-person operation run on credit cards into a firm with a steady flow of new clients. Instead, I was so stressed out I couldn't sleep. I hated going into my own office every morning.

And no wonder. That office was a nightmare. I spent most of my time there putting out fires between my employees. As soon as I'd resolved one conflict, another would flare up. It was all internal battles, workflow disruptions, grumbling employees, high turnover, and even instances of theft.

Instead of taking charge, I began consciously trying to avoid being the first person in or the last person out of the office. The more I could avoid being at my desk, the better. I'd come up with excuses to be late or stay away entirely. Any reason was good enough to be away from that mess.

Reviewing all the day's problems each evening, I couldn't work out what was going wrong. I kept thinking to myself, *This is the greatest place to work in the world. Why doesn't everyone else feel that way?*

Deep down, I knew I had it wrong. TorkLaw wasn't the greatest place to work. In fact, it was hell, not just for me but for my employees. And though I had some toxic people in the office, that toxic atmosphere wasn't on them. It was on me. I'd failed to take charge at my own firm. And it showed. Every single day.

WHO'S IN CHARGE HERE?

The reason my firm was spinning out of control had nothing to do with my growth strategies, my advertising, or the revenue and reach of my competition in the city. It also had nothing to do with my skill as a lawyer. It's true our growth was stalled and the competition was fierce, but those were symptoms of a larger problem: I felt like I was already doing enough. I felt like by hiring people with the right qualifications (at least on paper), winning cases, and spreading the word about the firm, the firm should basically run itself.

Essentially, I left a void in the firm where the leader should be, and the wrong people stepped in to fill it. In particular, it was Patricia who ruled the office. She was my best paralegal, an absolutely outstanding worker. She was experienced. She knew the process better than most lawyers. To this day, I still haven't seen a paralegal better than her. She was fast, responsive, good with the clients, and she had the technical knowledge to execute on whatever task I gave her. Every month she blew past her targets and went above and beyond anyone else in the office.

From my perspective, she was flawless. By far, she was my most valuable employee. As far as I was concerned, she was the best person to take the lead when I was too busy to attend to day-to-day management.

So when others would complain about her behavior, I naturally took her side. I chalked it up to jealousy and pettiness on the part of the poor performers. When I heard her called manipulative or mean, or when she was accused of setting people up to fail, I thought it was ridiculous. When employees said, "It's her or me," I'd fire them. How dare they give me an ultimatum at my firm!

Reading this, I'm sure you can see my mistake, but in that moment I thought I was acting properly. Patricia had given me no reason to suspect her, and I didn't see any reason to indulge those who couldn't produce at her level consistently. I was trying to build an elite firm. I didn't have time for their problems.

It wasn't like I personally mistreated anyone. I was kind and respectful to every employee. I simply made it known that my rationale was that the numbers were what mattered, and Patricia delivered on the numbers. As far as company culture went, I demonstrated politeness and hard work, and I expected everyone to deliver the same.

Wasn't that enough?

Clearly not. In fact, this approach had made me part of the

problem. Instead of stepping in, digging to the root cause of all the dissatisfaction amongst the employees, and bringing an unbiased approach to office disputes, I checked out, refused to listen to personal issues, and simply took Patricia's side. Despite my attempts at politeness, the culture I was really demonstrating was indifference and favoritism—and the staff were definitely delivering that right back to me.

Things got so bad that I later found out that the office developed a meme about Patricia and I, in which she played the part of Grima Wormtongue and I was King Theoden from *The Lord of the Rings*. I was, theoretically, in power, but Patricia was always in my ears, directing my choices.

If I'd known more about *The Lord of the Rings*, perhaps I would have taken some solace from that. Theoden is, after all, a good and decent man. He simply stopped leading his people and let the malicious Grima frame every decision for him.

In fact, Theoden would go on to become a good leader again—but only after he took control back for himself.

WHY FIRMS STRUGGLE WITH LEADERSHIP

Law firms often end up struggling with leadership issues like those I had at TorkLaw, partly because of the evolution most of those firms undertake. For most firms, initial growth is slow and requires a very small team. Early on, the firm is just you. Then it's you and a couple administrators. Perhaps you bring in a lawyer or two. At that point, you are still able to have direct, personal control over everything that happens at your firm. There's no need for a vision or a clear voice that represents firm policy because you are still doing or overseeing everything yourself. You know every employee well, and they know your vision through their constant contact with you. You speak to every client, so every client knows the voice of the firm.

As soon as you scale even slightly larger than this intimate setting, though, it becomes impossible to maintain that direct influence over everything, and a lack of leadership begins to become noticeable. Ignoring those early signs of trouble allows the leadership vacuum to grow, until you end up with a Patricia in de facto control of the office culture.

While this often occurs at Stalled firms with a reasonably large staff, it can happen even earlier. If you run a False Start firm, you can easily become so distracted by efforts to grow that you don't develop those strong individual relationships with your small staff that would take the place of executive leadership. While you're chasing potential clients, the firm can drift far from your intentions.

One way or another, the lack of leadership eventually makes its absence known. Where there ought to be a determining vote on tough calls, there's silence. Where there's conflict between priorities, it goes unresolved. Where friction arises between team members, the temperature is allowed to keep rising.

The behavior you exhibit and tolerate and the standards you refuse to set ultimately become the fabric and composition of your culture.

Looked at this way, the solution becomes obvious: you have to fill in that gap in leadership.

PARTNERS ON THE SAME PAGE

Of course, not every firm that hits the False Start or Stalled stage has only one potential leader. Often, these firms are partnerships with two or more lawyers in a position to take control and move the firm forward. Unfortunately, when setting a course for a business, two heads are not necessarily better than one.

Far too often, partnerships are founded with a critical misalignment in vision. Put simply, the partners simply don't agree on what the goals are for their firm. A business partnership is like a marriage. To be a success in either, you need alignment in values and goals for the future. Any time there are differences on those core points, there's tension. A marriage in which one person wants to live in a big city and prioritizes high-paying positions with long hours is going to run into trouble if the other person wants to live in the country and put more time into having a big family.

The same is true of your firm. If you have a partner who wants to pull money out of the firm in order to take time off and travel regularly, that isn't going to work long term if you believe in reinvesting to scale. If you want a firm in which everyone in the office is focused on achieving the most possible success and your partner just wants to be left out of it, neither of you are likely to be satisfied with the office you end up with.

Under those circumstances, it might be best to consider parting ways and starting a new firm on your own. I speak from experience. I left a firm I founded with partners precisely because we had different visions for the future of that firm. Someone was always going to be unhappy and unwilling to accept the chosen direction, so it was much better to separate.

To be clear, I am not saying that a partnership should be free of disagreements. Disagreements in marriage or in a business partnership are good; it's a matter of what those disagreements are about. Having different goals is a problem, but having different perspectives on how to achieve the same goal is excellent. There are plenty of roads available in order to reach whatever achievements you have in mind, and having those debates are incredibly valuable—but you have to be in agreement on where you are going.

When you do have that general agreement on purpose, a partnership can be extremely rewarding. Consider the rise of Apple under founders Steve Jobs and Steve Wozniak. Jobs and Wozniak were extremely different types of people. Jobs was a conceptual perfectionist. He came up with incredible ideas and could see the direction technology was moving, but he didn't often get his hands dirty working out the practical side of his ideas. That's where Wozniak came in. He was an engineer who could take the concept and turn it into a real computer.

In a law office, this dynamic may manifest with one partner developing the standards, direction, and growth strategies for the firm while the other enforces those standards, pushes that direction, and implements those strategies in the office.

Again, though, the Jobs and Wozniak partnership only worked because both of them wanted Apple to be the biggest computer company in the world. If one of them had simply wanted to build a computer they could sell to IBM and retire at thirty, their company would have fallen apart.

There's nothing wrong with wanting to get rich off of one big idea and spending the rest of your life on a beach, of course. No one is in the wrong if partners don't agree on a general vision. But that disagreement should be a deal breaker. To run a successful, growing business, everyone involved has to sign up for the same thing. Otherwise, clear leadership is impossible. And, again, without that leadership, the firm will continue to struggle.

EMBRACE YOUR TRUE ROLE

One thing the folks on Wall Street know that lawyers don't is that a business requires leadership just as much as it requires talent. A baker who makes the best cakes in town will see their bakery fail if they are incapable of managing their team properly. The same will be true for a brilliant real estate agency, repair shop, or school—no matter how talented the founder, failure is inevitable if they can't lead the rest of their staff.

In other words, as the head of your law firm, you (and any partnership you have) must recognize that you have to take ownership of every problem in the office. Let me repeat—every problem belongs to you. Taking complete and total ownership of all the problems is the only way to fix them and move forward. The worst thing you can do in these situations is shrug your shoulders as I did or assign the problem to someone else.

There are many potential solutions to such problems at your disposal, but *you* have to take advantage of them. Sometimes, it's a matter of reassigning a team member who clashes with others or doesn't quite fit their current role. Sometimes, the situation requires retraining. Other times, you have to let the person go.

Of course, taking any of these steps is a really hard thing to do.

No one likes telling another person that they aren't good at their job. It's an extremely unpleasant experience to fire someone. To this day, I feel terrible whenever I have to make that call.

Far from this being a drag on your other priorities, office management *is* your priority. This is what you sign up for when you open a law firm. It isn't just a matter of putting your name on the door and signing the checks. Running a firm requires you to take accountability for everything that happens in your office, the image of your firm in the community, and the experience of everyone who interacts with it. You aren't just accountable for winning your cases. You are accountable to your team, your clients, your family, and yourself.

Whether you like it or not, by taking on this role, you have chosen to be responsible for the whole of your firm, and if you want to turn your firm into a success, you have to start embracing your role as the CEO. And to succeed as a CEO, you need to understand what that role entails.

Ideally, a CEO isn't concerned with the petty conflicts between individuals at a firm. Issues like those in my office crop up because the leadership role has been empty for too long. When handled more successfully, a CEO can focus on their core directives:

- To create the vision for the business and the core values that center it.
- To ensure that everyone—top to bottom—is committed to doing the work required to move things in the right direction.
- To become the voice of the firm in how it speaks to the public.

- To provide clear, decisive leadership whenever new problems arise.

This is the type of comprehensive guidance that firms are often missing. By embracing your role as CEO, you can *actively* address the weaknesses in your firm and build a business environment where like-minded, dedicated, hard-working people come together to serve clients, make an impact, and scale to the zenith of your ambitions.

You don't need the guidance of an executive from Wall Street. You can make those changes yourself.

THERE'S WORK AHEAD

Whether you are a sole practitioner or part of a partnership, taking up the role and responsibilities of the CEO is a daunting task—one we often try to push off as long as we can. When we take an honest account of ourselves, we often have to admit that we are the ones holding our firms back. We are the reason the firm isn't living up to the standards we'd hoped to set.

That was the position I had found myself in at my own firm. Because I had refused to engage in the disputes between my employees or set and enforce standards that would have avoided those disputes, I had allowed Patricia, along with several others, to corrupt my vision of an efficient office with a positive work environment and turn it into the exact opposite.

To take control back again and place myself in the CEO role was going to take work. The first thing I had to do was face the immediate, pressing issue with the toxic environment in the office. Instead of trying to avoid coming in, I had to step up and take the situation on directly.

My chance came when Patricia entered my office one day saying one of my attorneys wouldn't review her work. This seemed like an outrageous claim. Instead of simply taking her word and empowering her to deal with the problem—as I might have in the past—I told Patricia to take a seat while I called the attorney in question into the room.

Once they were both settled, I asked my attorney point blank, "Patricia says she has all these items that require your review and approval and that you're refusing to do that for her."

I've never seen someone look more confused.

"What are you talking about?" he asked. "There's nothing in my queue right now. What did you send over?"

I turned my attention to Patricia, whose mind was clearly working furiously trying to find an exit plan.

"Never mind," she said eventually. "I must have been mistaken. I think it'll be okay."

It was like seeing her for the first time. The scales had fallen from my eyes, and there sat the person that I'd heard about so many times from others in the office. The person who had been so attentive and friendly with me, the person who had always hit her targets, the person who I thought had represented precisely what I wanted from my employees—she had been playing me for months.

"Thanks," I told my attorney. "I think that'll be all."

I asked Patricia to remain behind.

I can't say I was happy to let Patricia go. I was losing the best earner, and I was also conceding to my own failure as a leader in my firm. But in that moment, I also took control of my firm back. I accepted that any change had to start with me.

It was my job as an employer to provide stability and protect my people. It was my job to not just set an example but create a structure that would enable my employees to work in a positive environment.

If I had been a CEO of a publicly traded company, I probably would have lost my job by that point. Luckily, I wasn't. I couldn't be fired. But if I wanted to see things change, I had to start making those changes myself.

And as I sat there mulling over the new future for my firm, I realized where I had to start. If I wanted to have an office I enjoyed going to—an office focused on success at the level I expected—I needed to start by changing the culture.

PART II

BUILDING YOUR CULTURE

CHAPTER 3

FIND YOUR WHY

There's a story I've always loved about John F. Kennedy. Back in 1962, shortly after President Kennedy had famously vowed that the United States would go to the moon by the end of the decade, he went down to Houston to tour the NASA facilities and see how development was progressing on his ambitious target. While taking a tour of the immense premises, he approached a janitor who was busy at work.

Kennedy held out his hand and said, "Hi, I'm Jack Kennedy. What are you doing?"

"Well, Mr. President," the janitor responded, "I'm helping put a man on the moon."

I don't know if that interaction ever really happened, but I love the message behind it. It speaks to the profound power a great culture can have on everyone in an organization. It must have been so easy for the engineers and astronauts at NASA to feel that kind of incredible purpose behind their work. They knew they were part of a historical, world-changing team. What's amazing, though, is that the NASA culture was so powerful even the janitors in Houston felt it.

And why shouldn't they? It would be pretty hard to develop the technology, practice the flight skills, and work out the math to get to the moon if the trash was overflowing and the toilets were all backed up. The janitors at NASA *did* play a key part in that organization's success. They had every right to feel that pride in their work.

When you think about it that way, what is striking about this story isn't how the janitor felt about his job, but how rare it is for an organization to provide that same type of purpose to their entire team. Why is it that so few companies make sure *everyone* feels that sense of purpose in their work?

WHY YOU NEED A "WHY"

When you realize that your firm stalls or experiences a false start and doesn't initially succeed on the scale you intended, you may conceive of any number of strategies to address this shortcoming. You could expand into other areas of law or find a niche focus and become the law firm to address that particular legal issue. You could hire a marketing team to adjust your advertising or change your branding. You could hire (or fire) more staff.

These are all valid considerations, but before you overhaul the entire firm, you can start with a basic question: why are you here?

I don't mean that in some cosmic sense; I am being very practical. Why does your firm exist? Why did you start it instead of finding a job at someone else's firm? Why should anyone else want to work for you, and why should clients come to you for legal assistance?

In law, we often skip over these questions. You have a firm because you're a lawyer. You're there to practice law. That's the extent of your purpose.

Ask any successful business outside of the legal industry, and they'll tell you the same thing: these shallow explanations are not enough to build success upon. If you want your firm to rise above the competition, your firm has to stand out. It has to represent your personality, your beliefs, and your motivations. And to put those concepts into place, you need a "why" that expresses your vision for the firm and a set of core values that anchor every choice you make.

This is not a radical point. Every business listed on the New York Stock Exchange needs to have a vision and core values. That conceptual framework is key to grounding a company and providing it with purpose. For some reason, though, lawyers feel like this doesn't apply to their firms.

It absolutely does apply, though. At heart, you have to give employees and clients a reason to buy into your firm. No one else is in your head, so no one understands your passion, purpose, or dedication if you don't explain it to them.

The reason your "why" has to come first is that everything else in your business flows out of it:

- How you treat employees.

- How you expect them to treat one another.
- How you motivate your employees.
- How you treat clients.
- How you communicate with clients.
- How you describe your firm in advertising.
- What technology you invest in to strengthen your firm's priorities.
- The direction you hope your firm is moving.
- How your team can help move things in that direction.

Without a "why," all of the decisions you make that influence these priorities will be aimless. For you, decisions will be a matter of whim or gut instinct. For others, it'll be a matter of guesswork, trying to fill in the blanks because you haven't explained your reasoning to anyone.

Your firm is like a person. It needs a personality, it needs purpose, and it needs direction. It needs continued nurturing and improvement. That won't happen on its own. Your firm won't suddenly develop these qualities because you're walking around the office. They require a great deal of thought, careful wording, and consistent implementation. That's the formula for bringing a Stalled or False Start firm back to life.

FINDING A VISION

I founded two firms without ever developing a "why." I didn't know I needed one. I knew that I had become a lawyer because I wanted to help people, and I thought that motivation would simply wear off on people. We've already seen where that kind of thinking led my office.

It was only when I realized that I had to truly take charge that I saw how the lack of any "why" to bring people together had helped lead to a fragmented, divided office. How could anyone know what kind of behavior was expected when I didn't offer any rules or reasons to guide them? Perhaps more importantly, how could I know what behavior I was modeling without setting my own guidelines?

I thought I was showing my team how to behave properly, but really, I was sending mixed signals. On the one hand, I acted kindly in one-to-one interactions. On the other hand, I rewarded the worst behaved members of my team. What were my employees meant to take from that example? What could they draw from that display to show them how to conduct themselves and what was expected?

Those were the questions I was facing, and I realized that taking a leading role in the firm wasn't going to be enough. I had to give the firm a "why" simple enough for people in the office and clients outside to understand what we were doing there. If we weren't just there to make money and go home, what were we doing? Who were we? How did we intend to act? What did we prioritize? Where were we trying to go? What was the point of this firm?

To carve out that "why," I determined I needed two things: a vision for the firm and a set of core values that could guide our actions.

To develop that vision, I started with the basics. We're a personal injury law firm. What does that mean? We represent those who have been harmed so that they can get compensation for what happened to them.

These are objective points, but a vision has to be subjective. It's personal. So I started digging deeper. Why is personal injury work important to *me*?

Without us, our clients would have no chance against the behemoth corporations whose job it is to stand in the way of just and fair compensation. We play an invaluable role in standing up for them and providing justice.

And why is that role important to me?

Because we can change people's lives.

It was startling to realize it. This was the deep motivation that had pushed me forward into starting TorkLaw. While I was ambitious for success, at root I wanted that success so I could change the lives of as many people as I could. That's what I loved about the job. We could change lives. Every day. From the moment a client comes into our office on their darkest day to the day their case is resolved, we are changing their lives.

That's as compelling a vision for a firm's existence as any I've ever heard. I can't imagine a more fulfilling thing to do with your life. And what's more, it was honest and authentic. I felt that drive deep inside me. It was my own motivation for this work. I'd simply never put it into words.

With a vision in place, I could communicate directly and specifically what this firm stood for. And I suddenly had a purpose that I could hold myself accountable to. If I wasn't serving the vision of helping TorkLaw change more lives, I needed to adjust my behavior. Because that was what mattered at my firm.

THE CORE VALUES BEHIND YOUR "WHY"

Having a vision for your firm is extremely valuable, but it doesn't really codify how people should behave in the office. Vision provides a purpose that can motivate everyone from the top lawyers to the janitor, but to help people live up to that vision you need a set of core values that grounds your process and the culture of your firm.

To create an office culture that matched the ambitious directive of my vision, I had to reverse engineer values based on my experience of where the office culture had already gone wrong and where we needed to be. Surveying my team, I saw some people who weren't bothered about whether or not our firm was bringing in more new clients. So long as they did enough to keep their jobs, they were content. We'd also obviously had issues with lying and deception among team members and a real lack of respect for one another.

To live up to a vision of doing everything to change people's lives, I needed my staff to be direct. I needed them to say what they meant. And I needed them to stand by what they said.

Perhaps most of all, I needed everyone to feel that intense desire to succeed—on a personal level and on the level of the entire firm. We had to be a team, and as a team, we needed to fight our hardest so we could all be successful.

With these points in mind, I crafted solutions based on the core values that I believed in and that would allow us to scale and succeed at the highest levels:

- **Growth mindset:** This core value went far beyond simply helping the firm scale; it demanded that everyone attempt to reach higher for themselves. If TorkLaw was going to live up to its vision of changing ever more lives, we would have to strive to improve, take risks, and build upon our successes. I wanted to see every employee expect more from themselves in their work.
- **Radical authenticity:** To exorcise the gossip and backbiting, I instituted a policy that required people to be direct and honest with one another. Problems that had festered in whispers could now be cleared in the light of day. This would also limit the ability for a new Patricia to cause continual havoc.
- **Respect for one another:** I've always lived by this idea, but it wasn't enough for me to model it. I needed everyone to know that it was expected in how they interacted with one another and with our clients. Everyone in our office was deserving of respect. There could be no exceptions. This would help feed the directive to be authentic and honest with everyone. After all, if you respect someone, you can't gossip behind their back.
- **Unwavering integrity:** This one was for me as much as anyone. I needed to start living up to my words and intentions. My experience with Patricia had left me shaken. I couldn't help but run through all the times I'd told the team, "I care about you," and failed to live up to it. There had to be accountability for promises and expectations—for me and for everyone else. The new rule would be that if a promise was made, it would be kept, whether that involved a

commitment to be an impartial arbiter from the boss or a commitment to call a client back. From now on, we'd be a firm that stood by its word.

- **Ownership:** At TorkLaw, ownership would become more expansive than simply accepting the responsibilities that come with the job. Ownership, as I would define it, was more than just living up to the bare minimum; it was doing whatever it takes—being creative, taking chances, and going the extra mile. It involved each team member learning and allowing themselves to be uncomfortable sometimes. I had to shake the office out of its comfort zone where we were all just getting by. If we wanted to improve, we all had to own our responsibilities and do a little more.

- **Striving for the win:** All of these values came together in our desire to always win. This was more than looking to grow or doing a little extra; it involved coming together as a team to succeed at every opportunity. I founded this firm because I wanted to run a motivated team who believed in helping others. That's the value that was needed to bring this list together.

With these core values in hand, I gathered all the leaders in the firm together and presented my list. I made it clear that these were not just core values for what happens inside the firm, but in how we interacted with everyone. That included being respectful and showing integrity when working with opposing counsel, and being authentic and honest with our clients—even when that was uncomfortable.

Further, to solidify the place values would have in the firm, I created a system that would keep them always at the forefront of everyone's mind. Every day, we would review the core values.

We would also discuss revising the rules where necessary, allowing them to evolve with the firm.

Everyone would participate. Everyone would know our vision and values. And everyone would know the part they had to play.

RECOGNIZING OTHER PURPOSES

The change a "why" made to my firm was immense. Not only did it start to transform some of the performances in the office, it provided a metric by which to judge everyone who worked at the firm. It also made it possible to bring in new people and fit them into the culture even before they were hired.

This vision and these core values have worked wonderfully for TorkLaw. Through them, we were able to move from a Stalled firm to a true success. However, our "why" isn't meant to be copied and pasted over to your firm. While the work is the same, the particulars have to be different because this is *your* firm that has to follow *your* vision and *your* values. Perhaps my conception of my firm's place in the world and the values I try to live by seem unreasonable to you. Perhaps you care more about being part of a social dialogue on justice and arguing cases in front of the biggest courts in the country, changing laws as you go. If that's the case, then those priorities should center your firm, and your values should grow out of that motivation.

The power of these ideas comes from codifying what you believe in so that everyone who interacts with your firm knows precisely where they stand and what is expected of them. With that in mind, it's important to open the discussion of your "why" to others in the firm. After all, they are expected to live by it as well. A firm is bigger than you, and the ideas behind it have to provide purpose for everyone who works at your firm. In other words, your "why" has to also give everyone else a "why" that inspires and motivates them.

This is how you get everyone to buy into the values you establish, from your lawyers to your receptionists. Like the janitor at NASA, a receptionist is among the most important people in your office. They are the face of your firm, and they can make or break your image. If they haven't bought into what your firm is and don't feel pride in their position, what does that say about your firm to your clients or new hires?

Just saying "give good customer service" to a receptionist isn't enough. That customer service has to mean something to them. There have to be concrete ideas behind such concepts that they, too, believe in.

So seek out your team's thoughts on your vision and your core values. They may not be in a position to set your firm's "why," but let them know that their input is important.

Of course, whether invited into the process of defining your firm's "why" or not, some people simply will not believe in what you stand for. For some people, a growth mindset is meaningless. Some people don't want to go the extra mile for clients and teammates. And you can't build a business with such values if the people in the office don't agree with them.

That's why, once you've developed a "why" that you want everyone in the office to believe in and follow, you have to make sure the people fit the ideas. And if they don't, it's time to find new people.

CHAPTER 4

AN OFFICE OF TRUE BELIEVERS

I wish I could say that the toxic atmosphere in my office ended with the removal of Patricia and the installing of a "why" through our new vision and core values. Unfortunately, it wasn't that simple. Once I started looking more closely, it became very clear that there was more than one toxic person in the office. Patricia may have been the most obvious culprit, but she wasn't alone. Many of the people on my staff were simply never going to live up to the standards I wanted for our firm. Their behavior may have been less outrageous, but they still weren't aligned with the beliefs I was trying to set.

I realized that to truly move the firm forward and set it on a course for success, I was going to have to take dramatic action. In fact, I was going to have to risk the entire firm.

Shortly after I developed our firm's "why," I brought the whole staff together for a meeting at the end of the work week. In that room I knew there was a mix of people, some of whom could be assets on the journey ahead, others who needed to go. I just didn't yet know who fit in each category.

But I was ready to find out.

"I want to offer all of you a choice," I told them. "If you want to stay with this firm, there will be a lot of changes in the next few months. We'll be taking on new challenges and working harder than we have ever worked before. If that doesn't sound appetizing to you, and you want to leave today, I am ready to pay you three months' severance.

"This offer is available to everyone—no questions asked. If you want to leave, tell me today. You can have a great summer, enjoy your free time, and relax knowing you have a financial cushion in place while you find a new job.

"This offer is open to everyone, but I need an answer now."

My speech was greeted with silence. I knew that many of the people in that room were mulling over the offer. Was it worth it? Was it a trick? No one wanted to be the only one to raise their hands and accept it.

For my part, I was prepared to let everyone quit—even if that meant I had to start over again. TorkLaw needed a clean break and a fresh start. And I was ready to pay any price to get it.

In the end, more than half of my staff took the offer.

At the time, it felt like the worst thing that had ever happened to the firm. Little did I know that it was the most pivotal moment in our firm's history.

CULTURE ISN'T AUTOMATIC

Far from dooming my firm, letting those people go was one of the best decisions I've ever made. The reason for this is simple: you can't build a culture on words alone. It's absolutely critical that you create a unifying vision and put a set of core values in place, but if you don't have people who believe in those words, they're meaningless.

The only way to give those words the power to transform your firm is to ensure everyone in the office aspires to live up to them every single day.

It's been emphasized to the point of banality, but there is absolute truth in the expression "Your people are your most important asset." It's the people in the office who will make your culture. You can be an example of your vision and values, but you're only one person. For a culture to stick—and for it to begin to improve the growth of your firm—the consensus has to be there from everyone. Everyone has to buy in.

Now, if you are a solo operator running a False Start firm looking to hire your first employees and build a culture, you can implement the ideas of the last chapter without much difficulty. You're starting with a blank slate. Do the work on developing a "why" and use the strategies below to make sure you hire well. At that point, you should be on the right path.

If you already have a team in place, though, this is a bit harder.

At a Stalled firm, you have to start asking tough questions about who is capable of transitioning into the new culture you are creating.

This is not a task you can ignore or even put off. It has to be an immediate priority. If you don't make sure all of your people want the culture to stick, the toxic people in your office will continue to create your culture. It's only when you remove the toxic element entirely that a better culture can thrive.

Think about the experience of a new employee who is coming in for their first day after you have set down your "why." They walk into the office, and you sit them down to talk about the firm's vision and its core values. Great so far. You seem to live up to those values, and they have the impression this is a tough, honest, purposeful place to work.

Then they meet your staff. After your speech, you send them off for a little training. What do they hear from the people in the office during that training?

"Don't worry about this system. The boss never checks up on this stuff."

"You can probably half-ass this task."

"They really make us jump through hoops here."

Then they go off to lunch with the rest of the employees, where they learn even more about the values that underpin your office.

"This place sucks."

"It's just a paycheck. Don't take it so seriously."

"You don't really have to do much. Just look busy."

Not everyone agrees with these comments, but those who believe in the changes you want to make have learned by now to keep quiet. So there's only one perspective being shared at that table.

By the end of that first day, your new employee has definitely absorbed the office culture—but it isn't the culture you spelled out in the first ten minutes. In fact, they've learned that their boss—you—is completely disconnected from what the actual culture is. They've learned they can ignore you and laugh at you with the other people in the office. In fact, that's a better way to be a success in the firm than listening to you.

The only way you can break free of this cycle is to make sure all those employees whispering about the *real* firm culture are removed so they can't continue to influence everyone else. That's why implementing a new culture has to start with the people you already have.

Clearing away that toxic element in my own firm left me with a core group of people who I knew could take on our new culture. They were loyal to the firm and believed in the changes I was trying to make.

If I'd kept the entire staff on, those people who left would never have taken on the core values or vision. They would have shrugged it off because they didn't care. They would have laughed and rolled their eyes. And when they didn't change, that core set of employees would have followed their lead—or left to find a better workplace.

Instead, everyone who stayed proved ready to pick up the pieces and do what we had to do to fix the firm. There was no one laughing at our efforts, no one refusing to do the work. For the first time, the office was actually a team.

WHO FITS RIGHT NOW?

This leads to an obvious question: who on your staff do you keep and who do you let go? This may seem like a very difficult question, but in fact, it's as easy as admitting what you know in your gut. You don't have to line everyone up and offer them an ultimatum like I did. Unless you're running an enormous office, you most likely already know deep down who you should keep and who you should let go. You know who is participating, who is working hard, and who is acting with kindness and camaraderie toward their fellow employees. You also know who is slacking, who is causing problems, and who doesn't get along with the rest of the staff.

The problem, then, isn't sorting your employees; it's embracing your role as a CEO and doing the tough work of letting people go.

The biggest lie we tell ourselves as business owners is that we can change people. Let me clear that up right now: you can't. You can't teach a good work ethic. You can't teach someone a talent that they don't possess. If they don't want to change themselves, you can't make them. No matter how much time you give them or how much you care, if someone doesn't fit your firm's culture, that isn't going to change—ever.

The mistakes I've made with employees almost always come down to giving people too many chances—not too few. That may sound callous or cruel, but it isn't. I'm not saying the people I let go are bad people, but they didn't fit with what we were trying to do—and forcing them to fit would only cause more pain.

And I mean that. The people who pay the price for our indulgence in ill-fitting employees are your clients and the rest of the staff. Clients suffer when the work isn't done, and your employees suffer from the bad attitudes they're forced to deal with. You aren't really doing the person you're indulging any favors, either. It isn't much fun to constantly struggle in a position or feel uncomfortable with your company culture.

Delaying these decisions is false generosity. At root, it's about trying to avoid feeling like a bad guy. Instead, sending people on to a position that fits them better is the kind thing to do. Not everyone wants to work extra hours or grow a business. That's perfectly okay. Some firms are happy with standard procedure, and that person might be happier there. Meanwhile, at your firm, you should have a group of people who believe in the way you run your office.

This doesn't mean you should only give people one strike, but they don't need more than three. By choosing to own a firm and be its CEO, you are signing up for these tough calls. That means letting people go when they need to be let go. You can do this in a kind way. Be supportive. Offer fair compensation and assistance where possible. You don't have to be a jerk and tell them they're awful.

But you do have to get them out of your office.

HOW TO HIRE

Part of the reason I found that I had so many employees that didn't fit was because of my previous hiring policies. Up until my face-off with the toxic culture in my office, there had been little rhyme or reason in how I hired new employees. I'd post the job on all the standard job boards, get a thousand applicants, and hire whoever had a resume that ticked the right boxes and who said what I wanted to hear in the interview.

Of course, once someone has been through a few interviews, they usually figure out what you want to hear before you even ask the question. They can produce the right answers on cue. Since I was hiring for experience, anyone who got to the interview knew what to say to get the job. They knew how to play me. And many of them did, obviously.

This led to a constant cycle of hiring and firing. I'd bring in the wrong people, train them, discover they didn't fit the job, and let them go six months later. It was expensive, inefficient, and as we've already seen, horrible for company culture.

Now that I had finally cleared the office of toxic personalities, I knew I needed to develop a better way to hire so I didn't end up right back where I had been. To change my hiring process, I looked at how the best companies brought in employees and changed my perspective on what that hiring process represented.

Traditionally, most firms look at hiring as strictly a personnel matter. The only goal is to get someone qualified into the job. So they do what I always did: post the job, bring in the people with the most experience, and hire the best interviewer.

But the best businesses know that hiring is as much about marketing as it is personnel. When you post a job, you are marketing your company to potential future employees, and that should be reflected in what your posting says.

So the first change I made was to reimagine our job postings. Instead of simply posting job title, expectations, salary, and required qualifications, I transformed our job posts into advertisements for the firm. I included images of the firm doing charity work and being part of our local community. I added the list of our core values. I showed a happy, productive office, and I laid out our expectations in far more detail. This wasn't going to be an easy job, I warned, or an easy paycheck—but was going to be rewarding.

Essentially, instead of posting for every potential hire, I started marketing to the type of people I wanted to apply: smart, ambitious, hard workers who cared about their job and who wanted to change lives. To bring those people in, I tried to think about what the best possible candidates would find compelling about this place. What would make them choose my firm over another?

Changing postings to advertisements is such a critical step in better hiring because so often firms give the best candidates too little to go on. If you only list the job title, responsibilities, and pay for a position, you only give people one reason to apply: money. That's their deciding factor. If you're a smaller firm, you probably can't match the top salaries offered at your bigger competitors, and so you lose the best people to them.

In using traditional job postings, then, you're once again playing the big firm's game.

But you can compete on a different level.

Think about how Silicon Valley companies advertise for new employees. They play up the fun and creativity of the position. We ride scooters! There's ball pits and arcades! You'll be designing the software everyone in the world uses!

Those jobs also require really long hours and a lot of hard work, and they often aren't the best paying option for elite coders. Yet, all the same, almost everyone who can code wants to work at those companies.

This motivation isn't limited to Silicon Valley. Law firms are just as capable of creating compelling advertisements for their offices that speak to what the best candidates want in a workplace. And when you speak to those motivations, you can attract those candidates, even if you don't pay quite as much as the bland big firm down the street.

Once I had the right people intrigued, though, I still had a problem. How was I going to be sure that those top candidates made it to the top of the pile? After all, the dominant strategy when applying for jobs is to simply apply to everything. I was still likely to get the same thousand applications I always did, even if ten of those were now coming from stellar potential employees. How could I cut past the other 990 to get to those ten?

To solve this puzzle, I returned to what I wanted from the job applicant. Underneath all the core values I had laid out, there is an assumption that the people at TorkLaw are willing to work hard. After all, you can't have a growth mindset and strive for the win if you're only willing to do the bare minimum.

So if the job was going to require hard work, why shouldn't the application process reflect that expectation?

This is where the second big shift in my thinking came in. I decided I had to stop looking for reasons to hire someone and start looking for reasons *not* to hire them.

To start weeding people out, I began placing very specific instructions for how to apply right in the middle of the job posting. Again, most of the thousand applicants applying for a job aren't really interested in the particular job they're applying for. That job is just one of several they are applying to that day. It's a numbers game. They apply to enough jobs that, eventually, they get a call, get an interview, and get a position. To maximize their reach, these applicants apply on autopilot. They skim a post, click apply, and send over their resume with a carefully worded generic statement.

To avoid these autopilot applicants, the instructions I placed in my ad said that anyone applying directly through the posting would be automatically disqualified from the position. Instead, if they wanted the job, they had to call a number. If they read the ad carefully and called, they'd get a voicemail. On it, they would hear my voice telling them, once again, about the values of our firm and our belief in hard work. At the end of the message, they'd receive the name of an email account where they could send an explanation about why they were the right person, why they were a good fit for our culture, and what their salary expectations were.

With years of experience using this process, I can tell you with certainty that this simple system clears away the vast majority of application clutter. It's so successful because it catches autopilot applicants at every step. It catches the majority of applicants who click and apply without reading the application. It also catches the next-largest set of applicants who call but can't be bothered to email. And it catches those who email but don't follow the instructions in the voicemail.

By the end, the only resumes we actually see are those who buy enough into this specific position at our specific firm to follow the instructions all the way through. And even then we are still not done.

If those remaining candidates have the right qualifications, we send a link to a video interview with pre-populated questions. The applicant must then record themselves answering those questions and send it back. You'd be surprised how few of the remaining applicants send that video back in.

By the time we get the videos, we're down to the most motivated people who really want to do whatever it takes to work with us. When we watch the interview, though, we still aren't looking for compelling reasons to hire someone. We're still looking for reasons to weed people out. So we strike off the people who didn't care about what they were wearing in the video or who didn't put any thought into their background.

Once we are down to the final elite few who have done everything right, we have each one take a personality test and the Wonderlic comprehension test. Those tests give us a clearer understanding of each of our remaining candidates.

With that information in hand, we can finally choose the best fit for the firm.

It is no exaggeration to say that this hiring system has transformed the quality of the people who enter this office. Instead of just judging applicants on doing the bare minimum to apply for the job and the ability to charm their way through an interview, I know each person I consider is hardworking, dedicated, and motivated. I know they're conscientious and have the personality and comprehension skills to be a success.

At this point, hiring stops being a bet and becomes a science.

LAW IS A PEOPLE BUSINESS

Amazing as this may sound, five years on, every single one of the people who did not take the golden parachute offer I made that day has remained with the firm. Because I had a loyal core, I was able to concentrate on hiring the best people to fill our now-vacant positions. With the new hiring process in place, I could be confident that everyone who worked in my office knew they were expected to live up to our vision and core values every day.

Those features have become so ingrained that even when I do somehow manage to hire the wrong person for a position—after all, no system, no matter how well designed, is perfect—I don't have to fire them. The last few people who didn't fit our firm left on their own. Our culture was so strong and so ever-present, they felt uncomfortable. There was no one there to encourage their slack habits or cynicism. They were the odd person out. So they left.

I know many of you will say that these hiring and firing tactics only work in larger firms. You might be thinking that a False Start or Stalled firm can't do the same. However, when I put these ideas into place, TorkLaw was just another Stalled firm struggling to get along in hyper-competitive Los Angeles. If I could pull this off, you can too. If you have good values and communicate them to your potential future employees, you'll attract the type of people you want—even if you're a solo practitioner or a small partnership.

The truth is, above a certain wage, people will gladly choose to do work that they believe is important and valuable over a slightly larger paycheck. Purpose trumps pay all day across the board. That may not be true of everybody, but it is true of the committed, driven employees you want in your office.

Of course, even when you do bring in the best people, there's no guarantee that culture is going to continue to thrive forever. People lose focus, become disenchanted, and even the best sometimes find it tempting to game the system. In an era in which the office is becoming an ever more digital and abstract concept, it's far easier for culture to drift from its original vision and core values simply because the people responsible for that culture aren't in direct enough contact anymore.

That's why there's one more key to building a successful office culture: technology. Through the right technology we now have the capabilities of measuring and sustaining culture—even through a pandemic.

CHAPTER 5

CULTURE TECH

Metrics and data are incredibly important in my office, and one of the most important is our public record of accomplishment. Every lawyer is compared to their colleagues in terms of case work. The same is true for every paralegal and every assistant and receptionist. Each month, everyone in the office can see who is excelling, who is hitting their marks, and who needs a little help.

I didn't put this system into place to shame anyone—far from it, it was designed to be lauditory—but public accountability is a powerful thing. No one wants to see their names at the bottom of the list, particularly multiple months in a row. When you see that others are pushing themselves harder, it gives you motivation to do a little more yourself.

Motivation is only one benefit of the system. Additionally, it helps us find those people who don't quite fit our culture of striving for the win. If someone is regularly finding their name at the bottom of the list—and there are no compelling reasons for this happening—it becomes clear quite quickly that this may not be the office for them.

The real beauty of this system is that I don't have to say a thing to my team to keep them pushing to excel so they can measure up to our vision and core values. Nor do I need to say much to those who don't want to measure up. The culture polices itself—which is great news because it's no longer possible for me to be in every one of the TorkLaw offices (or home offices) policing it myself.

TorkLaw and its office culture now stretch across the country. For two years now, the employees of this firm have worked from home. Yet the "why" behind our firm's success is still going strong—thanks to technology.

NO RETURN TO "NORMAL"

Other firms used to laugh at me when I told them how much focus I placed on investing in technology. You're a lawyer, they'd tell me, you don't need to waste time and resources chasing the latest innovations. Even some on my staff thought it was overkill.

Why reinvent the wheel?

Why not stick with what already works?

Why strive to be the first to adopt some new platform?

At the time, perhaps this did seem more like an expensive quirk than a smart investment. We were among the first firms in Los Angeles to go totally paperless with our files. We did that more than a decade ago. We've been on a cloud-based phone system for years. Long ago, we moved most of our office communication from email to Slack and set up Zoom for distance meetings. Was all of this really going to help us outcompete the firms that kept investing in the traditional winners like billboard advertising?

I think I silenced all the doubters of this policy when TorkLaw was able to switch to a completely digital home office framework over lunch in March 2020 while the competition continued to scramble for weeks.

However, I don't want to claim any fortune-telling abilities here. I did not know that a worldwide pandemic was on the horizon and that my technology investments would help weather the safety measures put in place across the country. Instead, I invested in technology because it has always been clear to me that the concept of work is evolving in our society, and to keep up, we'll have to invest in the technology changing that conception.

This is why I dismiss the belief that office culture is ever heading back to what we currently consider "normal." Now that workers have discovered it's possible to work in more flexible conditions, and employers have seen they can spend less on office space, it's hard to imagine everyone will ever agree to going back to the forty-plus hour week spent entirely in the office.

While the idea of a future without offices seems to be overly dramatic, it's hard to see a return to the full-time office environment as the standard across most industries, including law.

So here is another prediction for you: with or without the

influence of private equity, we're heading for a new kind of work—and technology will have to play a major role not just in enabling that work, but allowing company culture to continue to thrive.

The future of work is likely a hybrid system, one in which there's a mix of in-office and remote work. Some employees will work in the office all week; others will work entirely remotely (from anywhere in the world); and others still will split their week between the home and the company office. This system is already a reality in some businesses, and over time, it will become the new standard.

If this prediction is correct, technology will have to do far more than it traditionally has at your firm. It will have to not only enable every employee to work within this hybrid system (ensuring access to all files and communication tools anywhere in the world), but also allow employers to track employee effectiveness—all while also building the culture that's so central to the future of law.

CULTURE-ENABLING TECHNOLOGY

If you can't keep everyone in an office and personally watch over the culture anymore, that doesn't mean you have to resign yourself to letting that hard-won culture dissipate. Despite the fact that culture necessarily requires human interaction, there are ways that technology can fill the gaps to allow that interaction to become digital. Done right, technology can even supplement our ability to create and enforce culture in person.

Some of these technologies are obvious. After two years of

at-least-partial remote work, we're all very familiar with apps like Slack and Zoom. However, there's more we can do with these tools than host digital meetings. You can encourage your employees to use Slack as a digital watercooler—sharing stories, videos, and photos, talking about the latest TV shows, and bonding through conversation. Zoom can also be used for more than stiff conference calls. At TorkLaw, we have virtual happy hours. With a requirement for everyone to have microphones and cameras on, we can create a sense of connection and interdependence that usually comes from face-to-face interaction.

But this is only the start. We also use online delivery services to bring our employees gifts at home. Sometimes it's an ice cream delivery. Sometimes it's cookies. Sometimes it's company swag. These little acts of appreciation can be scheduled digitally, and employees are always grateful to find a sweet sign of appreciation on their doorstep. Having staff outside the office doesn't mean you can't have a pizza party to lift morale. Schedule a Zoom call and have pizzas delivered to everyone's door. The options here are almost endless.

So technology clearly has the ability to provide the means to maintain connection and enable culture. We've also seen how it can be used to monitor productivity and motivation. But it can still do more. It can help you keep tabs on how thoroughly that culture remains ingrained through employee-to-employee interactions.

At TorkLaw, we've implemented a system that allows every employee to give away points to those who really live up to our core values. It works like this: Every month, each employee is given one hundred points. Those points can be given away in any number to any employee who does exceptional work while exemplifying our core values. If someone goes out of their way to take care of a client, for instance, others can reward them with points. If someone else is honest and direct in a very difficult situation, they can get points for that too.

At the end of the quarter, the employee with the most points gets a prize. Sometimes that's a nice luxury item, like a Peloton bike, other times it's a significant cash prize. We always make sure that the prize is sure to catch everyone's eye.

When you've already hired a bunch of winners, giving them this ability to recognize others and win something motivates everyone to buy into what this firm is about—whether they're in an office in California or Illinois or sitting at home. It also gives extra motivation to participate. As with our public record of accomplishments, no one wants to be seen as the only person who didn't share points or never gets points for taking part. Everyone is encouraged to highlight success from their colleagues, cheer each other on, and go that extra mile to earn points themselves. All of this is done through technology we have implemented into our existing systems.

To my mind, that's the best kind of culture a firm can have.

TURNING TOWARD CLIENTS

We've started this journey with office culture because culture is often the deciding factor in the success of any business, and law firms are no exception. Everyone in a legal office is doing work that is incredibly important to someone. Our work always has the potential to change someone's life. Winning a case can mean covering medical bills or receiving closure after an act of injustice. When we do our jobs well, we become an important part of a person's whole story. There will always be a before and an after they walked in our doors.

If people don't believe in that work—and if you don't have technology tools to strengthen that belief—there's little hope they can ever do that work successfully. Without the right people, the right culture, and the right technology, growth becomes extremely difficult.

We'll explore technology further in Chapter 7.

Now that you have a culture in place and the tools to enforce it, you can address some other concerns. These revolve around the oldest business cliche in history—the one that even lawyers have heard: "The customer is always right."

PART III

CONNECTING TO YOUR CLIENT

CHAPTER 6

MEETING THE MODERN CUSTOMER'S EXPECTATIONS

A number of years ago, my wife and I went to the Ritz Carlton in downtown LA to celebrate our anniversary at a new restaurant that had just opened. We booked a reservation and hopped in the car, excited for what we assumed would be a memorable evening. We definitely got what we expected—although not how we'd imagined it.

The evening did not start quite how we'd hoped. As I pulled up to the hotel, my car battery died. I was mortified, and what's more, I was worried. Remember, it was nighttime in downtown LA. That's not the safest of places for a car to break down. Would the Ritz Carlton have the car towed? Would they even let us in?

The valet, who must have been no more than twenty years old, seemed to sense my anxiety. He jogged up to the car and waited patiently as I apologetically explained the situation.

"Sir," he said, "don't worry about a thing. Go enjoy your dinner. We'll take care of everything."

I handed him the keys and left the situation in his hands. And I'm glad I did. While my wife and I wined and dined, that kid managed to find an auto shop that was open late and replaced the battery by the time we had finished dessert.

What is most remarkable about this story is that this wasn't some highly paid manager going the extra mile; it was a likely fairly low-wage employee at the bottom of the Ritz Carlton hierarchy. He simply knew the expectations for service at his place of work. He knew the service he should deliver, and he made sure to deliver it.

Now imagine if everyone in your firm had that same attitude.

LAW IS A SERVICE

When considering all the possible ways to attract more clients, lawyers very rarely consider the most straightforward basic business principle of them all: provide better service.

Far from heeding this advice, many firms seem to do quite the opposite. They run their firm like a motel and expect to attract clients like they're the Ritz. If you want to see those Ritz clients, you have to create a firm that lives up to those standards in the same way the high-end hotels always do.

Which One Are We?

Consider the simple act of taking and returning phone calls. So many firms don't return calls from potential clients. When a call comes in after hours or over the weekend, it goes to voicemail. Instead of racing to return those calls as soon as someone is back in the office, it can often take days before anyone chases that lead—if they do at all. By the time someone at the office does call back, that case is gone. One of their competitors picked it up in the meantime.

The lesson here ought to be the value of swift responses. Instead, it's seen as evidence that follow-ups don't bring in new clients, and little effort is made to improve the system.

And this is really only the beginning of the problem. Even when someone in the office does pick up the phone or return a call to a potential client still looking for a lawyer, their attitude often ranges from unenthusiastic to outright rude, with the occasional variation of simply not being very helpful. If anything, this gives an even worse impression of the firm than no response at all.

Lawyers feel they can run their firms like this because law firms have always been run like this. After all, this is why we have *clients* instead of *customers*, right? Customers expect service, clients get whatever we give them. Our work is so valuable and exclusive that people have to take what they can get from us. Our job is to win the case. Everything else is a luxury.

But we're no longer living in the 1970s when this was the standard for service across many industries. The clients of today are used to going online and getting near-immediate information or service whenever they need it. Google generates answers in an instant. Amazon delivers millions of items the next day with a click of a button—and increasingly more items the same day. UberEats and DoorDash deliver meals from any restaurant in thirty minutes.

Customers also expect to *always* speak to a real person when they call a company for information. When they have a problem with their Mac, they can call the Apple helpline at any time, day or night, and speak to an actual technician who diagnoses the issue right away and guides you to a solution. The last time I called my bank, the call was answered within two rings by a real person and the problem was resolved within two minutes.

There are lawyers and trial bar associations who are in denial about the sea of changes coming and are feverishly working hard to keep the status quo, but they can't hold former expectations in place. The people calling your office don't draw a line between the service they experience at those businesses and the service they expect at your firm. And sure, Amazon, Apple, Google, and Uber are all trillion-dollar companies (or close to it) with vast resources. But your client won't give you allowances for that. They know there's a standard of service they can get elsewhere. They expect you to keep up with the rest. And if you can't, they'll find someone who can.

THE STATE OF LAW SERVICE

Who will that someone else be? In some ways, that's the motivation behind this book. If venture capitalists do end up dominating our industry, it will certainly be in part because of poor office culture, but it's likely that the true leading motivation will be the poor record law firms have in providing customer service and access. Perhaps the easiest argument to sell to the state governments that would mull over the necessary legal changes is the fact that almost every other field has evolved with changing customer expectations and access, except law.

This is such a devastating argument because it's absolutely true. Everyone is raising their game—even in fields previously famous for poor service. The US Postal Service used to be the butt of stand-up jokes. These days, they can email you previews of what is coming in your mail and allow you to track your packages as they cross the country. Recently, I managed to renew my passport in fifteen minutes at my local post office. I set an appointment online, got an email confirmation, and when I arrived, went straight to the counter and started the process.

Doctors' offices are the same way. You can now book appointments online, schedule virtual appointments if coming in is inconvenient, fill in intake forms online or receive them in the mail to reduce wait times, and offer suggestions for improved service through customer experience surveys.

In a world in which every other industry is trying to improve the customer's experience, law intractability is all the more noticeable and galling. "We'll call when there's an update" doesn't sound as compassionate as you might think it does. In fact, it comes off as dismissive. As does the expectation that people will accommodate a lawyer's schedule and a lawyer's priorities for updates.

The old client system just won't cut it. Whether you like it or not, you need to treat your clients like customers—because everyone else across the marketplace already does.

This also represents an opportunity for you. While the more established firms continue to obstinately uphold the old standards, your Stalled or False Start firm can race ahead of the competition by taking the revolutionary step of putting the client's needs first.

PUT YOURSELF IN YOUR CLIENT'S SHOES

I don't doubt that many lawyers agree with the proposition that firms should be more customer-friendly. The question becomes how to implement new policies that prioritize the client experience.

On some level, if you have created a strong company culture, you are already on your way. The main adjustment you have to make is to turn some of your core values outward so that your culture includes a client-focused perspective. On a very basic level, you can codify the most important fact about your firm: there is no firm if there are no clients. This fact is so obvious, and yet, so often, lawyers and their staff lose track of it. Instead of focusing on the necessity of clients, firms come to see them as case files—as a list of details or a percent of the overall caseload, an opportunity for income or a chance to get some publicity—not as the people they actually are.

I don't want to imply you or your staff are purposely disregarding how your clients feel, only that quite often we forget to put their feelings first.

Your office culture must therefore encourage everyone to put aside other concerns and focus on the real people who come to your office facing real struggles.

If you're in personal injury or criminal law, this is very likely the worst moment of your client's life. They would not have come to you if something awful hadn't happened to them or someone they love. There's been an injury, a death, or a risk of serious legal consequences. And now they find themselves trying to navigate a system that they do not understand. The legal process is tense, confusing, and complex at the best of times—and to reiterate, these are far from the best of times for your clients.

Beyond simple gratitude and a call for empathy in your values, you can start using this perspective as a lens to review every process at your firm. For instance, what impression do your new clients get from your firm when they first walk in the door? From your perspective, you want efficiency in this interaction—get them signed up as quickly as possible—but what about from your client's perspective? Are you offering them enough reassurance and comfort? Does your office communicate that this is a safe place for them to reveal their worries?

What about updates on cases? How often are you communicating with your clients? Again, from your perspective, if you don't contact your client for six months, there's nothing to worry about. That's just how slow the process is. But to your client, it's an extended period of anxiety. They are sitting at home, every day, wondering whether they will ever be able to pay their medical bills or fix their house or get justice for a loved one who died in a nursing home. Is there a way you could send more frequent updates, even if there's nothing new to report?

And how about returning those missed calls? If a client can't get hold of you one afternoon, from your perspective, it's simply a matter of a busy schedule. You have a lot of cases! People have to be patient! But to your client, it's a sign you don't care enough to pick up and answer a question that could make all the difference in their lives. What can you do to make sure they don't get that impression from your firm?

With every choice you make in your firm, consider how your clients will perceive that choice. What is the best way to communicate a delay or setback in a case? How can you make sure the wrong person doesn't respond to an email with a question that is critical to a client's case? What small acts of kindness can you incorporate into your process to let your clients know you haven't forgotten them when things slow down?

These are basic considerations in every other industry. It's time we start coming up with answers of our own.

PUTTING ON THE RITZ

To get beyond introspection, though, we need a model on which to base our service. And to me, there's no model better than the Ritz Carlton. Think about how my wife and I felt when our car died on that LA night. Consider our relief after discovering how far the hotel's service went on our behalf. Imagine how many times I've told that story—and how many people are going to read it in this book.

That's the level of customer experience law firms should aim for. Like my night at the Ritz Carlton, going to a lawyer is a rare event for most people. It's something they will remember and retell for the rest of their lives. Depending on the service you provide, that story can go one of three ways:

- "They took care of me when I was desperate. I never had to worry about my case once I hired them."
- "It was fine. But I can't say they really cared if I was their client or not."
- "I wouldn't wish that experience on my worst enemy."

Crucially, none of these responses depend on the result of the case.

I've won millions for people who hated my firm and almost certainly never said a kind word about us after the case. I've also won hundreds for people and seen them become some of our best advocates.

That word of mouth is often what makes the difference in the growth of a firm. Not the billboards, not the TV and radio commercials—simple, positive reviews your clients share with their friends. Generating overwhelming positive experiences has built the reputation for the Ritz Carlton more than any commercial ever could. It can do the same for you.

So the question for you shouldn't be whether you should pursue service for clients as vigorously as the Ritz Carlton, but how you reach that level of service as quickly as possible.

And the answer to that question has to include technology.

CHAPTER 7

CLIENT TECH

When we conceptualize technology, we often think of big changes. We all love the sci-fi potential of new gadgets when they come out. Remember how exciting the first iPhone was? Or the FitBit? We still see this all the time in advertising. How many commercials have you seen talking about the incredible potential of 5G?

Yet sometimes the smallest advances are the most useful. At our firm, we have a CRM program that allows us to text our clients and save every text in the conversation. It all goes into the client's file along with all the rest of our communication. It's the absolute simplest, smallest feature you can imagine. And yet, it has made an enormous impact on our clients' experience.

We live in an age of texting. A lot of clients simply aren't comfortable talking on the phone anymore. They'd rather send a few words through an SMS. In some cases, it's simply less emotionally upsetting to type out those words than to vocalize their feelings. Other times, it's a convenience when out in public or at work. Whatever the reason behind the preference, texting allows clients to talk about their case in the way they prefer at a place and time that is convenient for them.

And by offering this service, we show that we want to make this process as easy and comfortable for them as possible. That's why we also have the option to send photos and documents through text. It's all about taking some of the stress out of their lives.

All of that may seem like no big deal to you, but using technology to place your client's needs first allows your client services to improve at the rate of technology. And as we all know, that comes at a blistering pace.

TECHNOLOGY IS THE BRIDGE TO CUSTOMER SERVICE

Many of the service expectations we covered in the last chapter that have revolutionized customer service are only possible for one reason: technology. Amazon is able to offer such fast deliveries because of technology and some really impressive logistics. 24/7 customer service has developed out of advances in worldwide phone services (improving the quality of international call centers) and automation. Even the valet at the Ritz Carlton may have only been able to find a battery thanks to the stellar quality of local search engine results.

Likewise, improvements at the post office and doctor's office largely revolve around advances in technology. It's technology that makes it possible to track packages and book online appointments.

The good news for you is that with a little investment, you can begin to provide similar levels of service at your law firm. With a quality CRM program and cloud-based filing system, you can see immediate improvements in how capable your firm is at handling client needs.

Technology makes it possible to do the little things a little better and offer real value. A slightly faster update, a slightly easier system to book an appointment, a slightly simpler communication system: these things add up to a big difference in how your client experiences your firm.

NEVER MAKE A CLIENT LEAVE THEIR COMFORT ZONE

Our CRM does more than allow texting, of course. It offers a variety of communication options to our clients. Along with texting, clients can call, email, or video chat. It's really all up to them. They can also access information on their file from their phones. The point of these communication tools isn't to impress people with our fancy technology; it's to create an environment in which the client can always reach out in whatever way is most comfortable for them. However they want to communicate and whenever they want to communicate, our app allows them to do it.

And this is just the beginning. We are debuting a new product at the end of the year that mirrors the advances in telemedicine in the medical industry. Current and prospective clients will have the ability to one-click connect with an attorney in real time via video on any platform.

This ease of connection is the most essential value you want out of client-facing technology: you make the client feel like you are there for them.

After an accident, an injury, some kind of injustice, or a combination of all three, your clients just want to know you care about them and what they are going through. They need to know that you care enough to do whatever it takes to make everything alright again. You can provide that reassurance by removing as much burden from their lives as possible and making it easier for them to remain connected to the process.

Why make them call your office on the phone? Let them live chat with you on your site.

Why make them come in to fill out their paperwork? Let them fill in and sign documents electronically from home.

Why risk missing an important date in their lives? Set reminders to send flowers after they get out of surgery.

When dealing with the pain and trauma of any situation that requires a lawyer, having fewer difficult tasks to accomplish is always appreciated, as is having more access to your lawyer, more updates about your case, and more signs of genuine care from your firm. With the right technology in place, you can deliver on all of those needs—and set your firm apart from the competition.

USE TECH TO BE RESPONSIVE

Comfort and care is important, but the biggest advantage client-focused technology gives you is that it allows you to be responsive to your clients. After all, having a direct line to the firm through text or a website doesn't amount to much if the response is slow and unhelpful.

This is a major problem for a business in any industry, but in law, a lack of responsiveness is a particularly significant issue. In fact, it's the number one reason law firms lose clients. Phone calls go unanswered, emails take days to return, and the questions running nonstop through a client's head remain unaddressed for what must feel like an eternity.

We've already looked at how some of this delay comes down to office culture and can be fixed through a culture adjustment. However, the problem with responsiveness at law firms often isn't a lack of interest in providing good service. The firm may well intend to be readily available and answer any question—during office hours, at least. But in an office in which hundreds of calls may come in every day, it can be difficult to source exactly who should field each call. Emails get waylaid and end up in the wrong inboxes. Somehow, clients end up talking to people who aren't on their case and don't have any useful information for them. To untie this knot, the client has to wait—sometimes thirty seconds, sometimes a few days.

Thirty seconds may not seem like that high a price to pay, but again, thirty seconds feels like a lifetime to someone who is desperate to get an update on the most important thing happening in their lives. You may know there's no news or nothing to worry about, but they don't. And they need to hear it from the person who knows their case. Every one of those seconds, they are wondering why their law firm cares so little about their case that the firm can't remember who is assigned to it.

All of this delay can be removed and the whole process simplified through technology. Automation technology can now funnel emails through to the lawyer directly responsible for the case in question. Phone routing systems can do the same, placing the call on the phone of the person who can answer the question. With digitized case documents, it becomes easier to access information and share it with clients, all while allowing everyone on the team the ability to connect to the case from anywhere in the world.

Where the traditional human factor has led to delay and confusion, automated technology can now result in far fewer errors with almost no time between the call or email and a response. Where traditional filing led to delays and misplaced files, digital documents are always only a click away. That allows a client to get the most up-to-date information on their case right when they need it.

CHECK YOUR SUCCESS WITH DATA

So far, all of these technology tools have been client-facing. Primarily, they make it easier to communicate with clients and share information on the case. However, there are other ways your office serves the client—such as the efficiency with which a case is worked—and technology has a role to play here as well.

Our firm uses a lead management system that logs cases from signup through to settlement, and having that data available has made a huge difference in how we connect to our clients. We've run advertising campaigns that have given us a false sense of accomplishment because all the obvious numbers are so positive. The campaign brings in a huge number of leads, and a very high number of those leads go on to sign up with our firm.

Digging further into the data, it becomes apparent that the

campaign isn't nearly the success it seems. We all know that dropped cases are part of the business, but only technology allows us to track if a particular campaign is bringing in more cases we eventually drop than they might normally.

Thanks to our lead management system, we know that most campaigns result in a few cases out of a hundred being dropped, but we've seen some of those "successful" campaigns with drop rates as high as 30 percent. That's a sign that we aren't reaching the people we can really help—and that's a problem. Luckily, it's a problem we can identify and solve through that technology.

This is the value of data in your technology. Through data, you can chart progress and correct mistakes as you refine every process to best serve your clients. When something—or someone—isn't working, you can put a figure on it and make adjustments.

Data can play a part in every aspect of a law firm. You can find out what procedures allow you to order medical records most efficiently and which lawyers on your team are receiving the highest satisfaction scores from clients. As a CEO, you have to recognize that every person and every process at your firm can improve—including yourself. Being able to put numbers on everything allows you to track progress and aspire to greater improvement.

Essentially, data lets the CEO know who is holding up the human end of client service, as well as where technology might be letting the firm down. It allows you to maximize effectiveness over busy-ness. To me, an employee who can execute on all their tasks in two hours is far better than one who stays "busy" for eight hours. In fact, if that employee can get all their work done in two hours, I want to know how they do it. Far from letting them go or demanding more busy-ness, I want them to teach me how they can be so efficient.

But I can only tell the difference between efficiency and slacking with the help of data.

LEADING THE WAY IN TECH

TorkLaw has remained at the forefront of technological innovation for law firms for one reason: I prioritized it. In my role as CEO, I set the course for our firm, and I decided long ago that smart investment in technology always pays off.

I'm sure there were other firms out there who would have agreed with that assessment back when I started investing, but they ran their firms on autopilot. It wasn't that they dismissed technology; it's that they never thought to take control and make that investment. As a result, their progress continued to stall or they never recovered from a false start, while TorkLaw has continued to grow.

At this point, 95 percent of our new cases are signed electronically—either through e-sign or text message. If we hadn't prioritized our technology, we'd still be signing clients by having them come into the office or visiting them. Technology has allowed us to sign up far more clients, and it has played a big part in the growth of our client numbers.

Whether it's culture, client services, or technology, this all comes back to your conception of your role and your willingness to act in that role to steer your firm. While another pandemic forcing us into a wholly digital workplace again is (hopefully) unlikely, disruptions and advances in our notion of work and customer service are inevitable. Investing in innovation means your firm can be the next one to be prepared for any contingency.

But that's only possible when you embrace your responsibility. As the founder and CEO of your firm, you are the business. Only you can make these investments—and only you can speak to what your firm is and can be.

PART IV

YOU ARE
THE FIRM

CHAPTER 8

ADVERTISE AUTHENTICALLY

Far too often, lawyers become so obsessed with hitting targets that we forget to take a step back and appreciate what we have—and what we're capable of doing.

I can be as guilty of this as anyone. After all, it's been my growth mindset and insistence that the firm strive for the win that has driven our success. But there can be a negative edge to that kind of thinking, a sense that no success, no matter how good, is ever good enough.

For that reason, I try to remind myself how very fortunate we have been at TorkLaw. While I am always driven to achieve more, we are in a position to provide help to people all across the country who come to us in moments of true desperation. They have been harmed, cheated, lied to, and dismissed by some of the most powerful actors in the world, and we have the skills, manpower, culture, and technology to help them fight back in a time of need.

Of course, most firms in personal injury will say something along the same lines. Personal injury is an extremely competitive industry, and everyone knows they're *supposed* to say something about how important it is to them to help their clients. What most firms forget to do, though, is show that they mean it.

That's why I never pass up an opportunity to prove that I mean what I say.

When the pandemic hit, it was a crisis—not for our firm, but for our community. This was a genuine concern for people in the TorkLaw office. Our firm culture is very community focused, and that culture is strong enough that everyone in the office wanted to do something to help.

So when we found out about the PPE shortage at local Los Angeles hospitals in March 2020, we decided to do something about it. We couldn't ignore the fact that while we were relatively safe working from home, the people who were saving lives couldn't protect themselves.

We started to buy masks to donate. Early on, when there were extreme supply chain limits, we had to pay far above a reasonable price per mask, but we happily put as much as we could toward them all the same. In the end, we donated more than fifty thousand masks over the course of the year, and we made sure they went to the hospitals that needed them the most.

We did that because we genuinely cared, but it was also the best possible marketing we could ever do. Instead of talking up how important our community was to TorkLaw, we showed everyone in our community that we meant it.

That's the kind of message you can never communicate on a billboard.

THE NEW MARKETING

In Chapter 2, we went over why you don't want to follow the standard law firm playbook that the bigger firms are using. Not only are their strategies, such as massive ad buys, extremely costly, they require a lot of investment to see reasonable returns. That kind of advertising only works if you have enormous resources to invest.

Most likely, you don't have those resources.

But even if you did, I wouldn't recommend putting all your advertising budget into generic billboards and commercials, because it is not clear that this model will remain sustainable for much longer, no matter the investment.

In case you haven't noticed, people are sick of traditional advertising. Thanks to the internet, we are now drowning in advertisements. According to the marketing research firm Yankelovich, the average person was viewing around five thousand ads a day back in 2007. Some studies suggest that number has already doubled. That's ten thousand ads every single day! And their impression of those advertising to them is often not particularly positive. Traditional legal advertising is as likely to earn a scoff as a call. In fact, it may lead potential clients to label that firm as ambulance chasers trying too hard to look impressive.

Expensive ad buys play into all the worst stereotypes about people in our profession. We're rich. We're greedy. We're out of touch. We'll say anything to get a client. We don't really care about anyone but ourselves. Filling the airwaves with your generic ads or putting your face on the side of every bus in town does nothing to counter all of these negative ideas.

Further, since you don't have a huge advertising budget, such an investment would also probably come at the expense of the more valuable improvements you could make in hirings or customer service—potentially creating a groundswell of negative reviews to go along with the suspicions raised by your advertising. Combining those two forces could slowly kill your firm. If you get a hundred clients from direct marketing and ninety of those people have bad experiences, how long will it be before those advertisements stop paying for themselves?

So what can you do? How do you get the word out there about your firm and what you stand for?

Live up to your values. And let people know about it.

PROVING LAW IS ABOUT MORE THAN MONEY

Providing PPE for hospitals was a moment of truth for our firm, a chance to prove to ourselves and to our community that we absolutely did care about more than attracting clients. The value of this choice went beyond morale. It provided clear proof to every potential client that we live up to the values we claim to hold.

And in my experience, that kind of proof always brings in far more business than a commercial.

The reason for this is because genuine acts of community service push so directly against the stereotypes we face as lawyers. Far from appearing like greedy ambulance chasers smugly grinning on a billboard, we show that we live up to the promises we make. We *do* care about the community. We *do* care about our clients. We *are* a team.

That also means we *aren't* a law firm that takes advantage of clients and does the bare minimum. We *aren't* one of those firms that won't return calls or give updates.

Every lawyer claims to be the best and claims to care, but very few firms ever provide the evidence that this is true. They think that displaying dollar signs of their big victories is enough. But that doesn't prove anything to most people other than one time you won someone some money.

Instead of trying to convince people of your integrity through a commercial, what if the way they heard about your firm was through a friend who knew what you stood for?

"Go with these guys, they got us PPE when the county was out."

"Check out this firm, they're downtown feeding the homeless every weekend."

"Try this place out, they took my brother-in-law's drug case for free and saved his life."

What we often miss as lawyers is that most people don't understand the law or what we do. They don't know that you got into this profession because you wanted to help people get some justice or financial compensation for injuries.

Trying to explain away this bias will fall on deaf ears—but showing them how you really feel can change everything.

At least, if you can get the word out.

SHARE YOUR GOOD DEEDS

Since traditional advertising has to be viewed with a little skepticism, the problem arises as to how you are going to share word of your good deeds—or indeed whether you should share them at all. Should you buy some radio time to brag about your charity work, or should you pretend it never happened?

Some people do great things and don't want to publicize it. We've all heard of anonymous donors who don't want their generosity to be made public. They don't want credit because they think it minimizes the value of what they've done. Or they worry they will look like they only gave because they wanted credit for it.

I don't want to criticize this impulse. I think that's an admirable position to hold, but it's not particularly tenable if you are trying to build a law firm. Remember, you're swimming against the prejudices of the average person who doesn't know you or your motivations. All they know is that lawyers are supposedly greedy and unscrupulous. If you keep your good deeds quiet, you are cutting off your very best avenue to disprove their prejudice.

So you have to make the proof public that you live up to your values and vision. But that doesn't mean you need to buy up more bus stop bench ads. The internet has provided you with an ideal advertising tool—social media.

Social media is a far more personal way to connect to your potential clients. It's a forum where conversation can take place. You aren't limited to slogans. You can post videos or write a few paragraphs to explain why your firm is different. It's also far cheaper than traditional advertising.

Everyone knows about social media, of course, but many firms still use it to copy and paste their standard advertising content. If you go on TorkLaw's social media pages, though, you will see far less of this traditional marketing and far more about our community involvement. When we donate food to a homeless shelter or sponsor a marathon, that's what we want to talk about because that's how we want people to think about our firm.

We live in the age of sharing, and at TorkLaw, we want to share that vision of what a law firm should be.

This strategy does more than just help us fight negative stereo-types or get our name out there; it allows us to advertise to the clients *we want*. In the same way that a job posting advertises to the type of employees you want to attract, social media posts can determine what type of client comes in your door. If the only thing people know about your firm is how much money you have won for your clients, you will attract people whose main motivation is getting money for whatever has happened to them—including plenty of people who are just looking for a payday.

In contrast, if you share your concern for individuals and your community, you'll attract clients who respond to those values—the type of people who are in genuine distress and need that care.

Just as your giving can attract new clients, it can also inspire your team. What better way to motivate them than to show in concrete ways how your vision and core values translate into concrete acts of good in the community where they live and work? You simultaneously prove that you stand by the "why" of your firm while giving them a reason to feel pride in their place on the team. While other firms may prioritize profitability, your firm puts community first.

At the same time, remember that the advertising you do for your future employees goes beyond job postings. Anyone motivated enough to jump through all the hoops of the elite application process at your firm will have first reviewed everything about your firm online. That includes what you post on your social media accounts. If your social media presence contradicts the values you lay out in your job postings, your best applicants may assume you don't really live those values in your firm. If all an applicant sees online is generic law firm advertising, they may assume you're a generic firm—however impressive the job posting. But if they see community service, a strong company culture, and examples of genuine customer service, they'll know your firm really is something special.

There's a final reason to share the good you do: it puts pressure on others to do the same. It may be that you are so high-minded that you'd rather lose the benefit of attracting more and better clients and applicants, and inspiring your team so that any act of public service is as morally commendable as possible. But keep in mind that anonymity also removes the pressure you can place on others to replicate the good you're doing.

If your firm grows because it develops a reputation for doing good, the next Stalled or False Start firm will know to do the same. And businesses in other industries may also catch on and start giving more. Your acts of giving can become a virtuous circle in your community—but only if you start it.

ALL MARKETING IS LOCAL—AND PERSONAL

This kind of modern marketing can be incredibly powerful in defining your firm. There's a reason the big companies listed on the Dow Jones create charities and work so hard to give their enterprises personality. However, there's one caveat here: you have to truly believe in what you're doing. Just as people have become skeptical of advertising, they've also learned to sniff out false piety. This is why no one associates those massive brands with their charities or assumes they do this for any other reason than some good publicity.

You can only break through this cynicism by genuinely pursuing causes that you believe in.

For a huge corporation, this is a major dilemma, but for your firm, it's as easy as choosing to make positive contributions that speak to your values. After all, as the CEO of your firm, you already have a culture that has set the foundations for this work. Your "why" lays out what you care about. Giving is only a further extension of this.

So where do your vision and values take you? What do you care about beyond the bottom line of your firm? It doesn't have to be hospitals and PPE. It can be any cause, so long as you are genuinely passionate about it.

Every firm has a different culture, and every firm founder has different priorities. As with everything in your firm, it all has to start with you. And that means you have to lead the way in creating the positive changes you want to see in the world.

This is obviously an exhausting and intimidating mandate. Far from the basic responsibility of winning your cases, being the CEO of your firm means you have to create values, live up to them, hire through them, connect to clients through them, and improve your community through them. That is no easy task—which is why truly taking care of your firm requires you to take care of yourself. Because without you, there are no values, there is no giving, and there is no firm.

CHAPTER 9

TAKING CARE
OF THE CEO

Like most people, I was terrified during the early stages of the COVID-19 pandemic. When the shelter-in-place order was announced, I was sitting at home, and my first thought was to protect my family to the best of my abilities. The virus seemed like such an overwhelming and incomprehensible thing. Back then, we knew almost nothing about it other than the fact that it was deadly and was spreading. How could I keep those I loved safe?

I knew that I had other responsibilities, as well. I wasn't just a husband and father. I was the CEO of TorkLaw, a person with a duty to take care of others. I thought of my employees scattered across the country, and I realized how terrified they must be. I owned my firm and had the financial resources to weather the months ahead. Their fears must have been even greater than my own.

I knew I had to do something.

I called every member of our team together for a Zoom meeting with one message in mind: I had to reassure my people. I told everyone on that call that their job was safe, and there would be no layoffs. No one was going to lose their position or see their pay cut throughout this experience. The one order I had for them was that they should take care of themselves and their families.

I could feel the relief through the computer screen. And I could feel something else: resolution and camaraderie. Once they knew I would step up for them, everyone else was ready to step up for the firm.

YOU HAVE TO BE ABLE TO LEAD

The loyalty I gained from that call played a major part in the success our organization had in 2020. I would confidently wager that my employees worked as hard as any at any firm in the country throughout the pandemic. Every TorkLaw employee put the firm first for the entire year.

They did that because I had proven that I had all of their backs. Just as our PPE donations helped demonstrate our genuine care for our community, standing by all of them in the COVID-19 crisis demonstrated that my belief in them and the firm wasn't just words. I meant it.

But I was only able to act so magnanimously because I had put myself in a position to offer that kind of reassurance. I'd made a point of taking care of the firm—and myself—so that I could take on the pressure and the risk involved in making the right choices at that moment.

Looking over our circumstances in March 2020, I knew we were able to pull off what I'd promised. The firm's finances were in a good place to handle any potential dips and unexpected complications. In part because of my suspicion of traditional marketing, we weren't overly burdened with expensive ad buys like some firms. We'd hired smart, so we had a lean, effective team in place. Our client loyalty was high, ensuring a continuing stream of incoming cases. And, of course, we had the technology to transition to a digital office and maintain efficiency.

In addition, I was in a good enough physical and mental place to put the concerns of my team first and recognize what they needed from me. Because I had taken care of myself, I could act on our firm's vision and change lives within my office.

DON'T BE A CEO STEREOTYPE

A well-rested, calm leader isn't the picture many of us have in mind when we think of a CEO. Instead, we're told through movies, articles, and anecdotes that success requires absolute sacrifice. If you aren't putting everything else to the side and devoting yourself exclusively to your company, you aren't giving your job your all.

We picture the CEO up at 4:00 a.m. after getting home at one that morning. He—because our conceptions of this position are almost always male—catches a meal when he can, and he has a portfolio at the table as he eats. His schedule is packed every hour, and there's never a moment free for a day off, let alone a vacation.

This austere stereotype is not only unrealistic, it's unsustainable for any human being. Even reported workaholic Tim Cook—who gets up at 3:45 a.m. every morning—still gets seven hours of sleep a night and takes time every morning for himself, during which he enjoys a work-free workout.

A study by Norwest Venture Partners in 2019 found that Cook isn't an outlier. Seventy-one percent of CEOs get more than six hours of sleep a night and 60 percent work out multiple times a week. They also found that most CEOs make a point of living full lives outside of the office. They pick up hobbies and schedule time for their favorite activities. They make room for quality time with their families.

These choices aren't made because these CEOs are soft and can't cut it—obviously. Instead, they all recognize that if you want to run a successful company, you have to take care of yourself first. If you aren't running your life effectively, you can't run your firm effectively either.

PROVIDING SELF-CARE

To be effective leaders in our firm, we have to absorb a basic fact of business: growth requires self-care. This self-care is not as difficult to accomplish as you might assume. A lot of it involves making sure you attend to the fundamentals of good health that you know already but simply don't focus on.

It all starts with sleep. Sleep is perhaps the most undervalued part of a successful person's day. If you aren't getting enough sleep, it drains your physical and mental reserves. It becomes harder to maintain concentration, make decisions, and remain empathetic through those long workdays.

After sleep, there's immense value in eating a healthy diet and working out. Even modest improvements here can net significant gains in energy. Moving around more, cutting out sugary drinks or fast food, and making sure you don't skip meals can provide you with the extra mental sharpness to pursue those exhausting changes your firm needs to undergo if you want it to scale at a faster pace.

You also need stress-relieving habits that can strengthen your mental health. These habits can take on many forms. Some people respond well to therapy. Others might meditate. Going for walks can also be valuable, as can reading as a means of escaping the concerns of the day.

And don't forget to take breaks. Pick up a hobby and schedule some time for it every week. It is also perfectly fine to take a vacation. Recharging means you have the energy to handle all those big problems when you get back.

Again, these are things you already know. Nothing here is revolutionary. But for many lawyers, the problem isn't knowledge, it's prioritization. If you want your firm to succeed, you have to prioritize your own health so you have the strength to push the firm forward.

MAKING HEALTH A PRIORITY

Health gets deprioritized by lawyers because it's so easy to dismiss as less immediately important than the problems they see right across their desk. When my office culture was so toxic, it was easy to see the fires I was putting out every day as more important than running in the morning or getting to bed on time. How can you focus on your diet when you have a trial date to prepare for or a new advertising strategy to implement?

Yet it is no exaggeration to say that health may be *the* reason you still have a Stalled or False Start firm. Poor health decisions affect how well you think and how much energy you have to implement the changes you know your firm needs. It's hard to create and integrate a company culture when you're tired all the time.

Health is not an extra you can put aside while you work on the firm; it is a critical part of growing your firm. Even in the chaos of a busy office when it can be hard to see an extra hour anywhere—you have to find that time for yourself. "I'm busy" is a very poor excuse. If something is important enough, you always make time. When a major case needs your attention, you move other items around in your schedule to accommodate. If you can find the time for a case, you can find the time for yourself.

THE EDGE

Like Tim Cook, I wake up early. For me, the day starts at 4:30 a.m. Also like Cook, I use that early morning time to work out because I know it makes me mentally sharper and gives me the energy to get through the day. I usually get seven or eight hours of sleep a night.

This is what the life of a successful lawyer-CEO looks like. It's these choices that have given me the ability to build a powerful and sustaining office culture, implement technological tools for the future, develop a framework that puts clients first in every circumstance, and share how much we care about our community as a form of advertising.

In other words, it's been my health, as much as anything, that has given me the edge over my competitors. It isn't just that I'm willing to outwork the competition; it's that I'm physically able to do so.

It took a lot of work to build a firm that doesn't have to constantly put out fires or assuage angry clients. If I'd always sacrificed my health to make that happen, I'd have a permanent case of burnout and my body would have given out years ago. Instead, I've developed a virtuous circle in which my efforts to strengthen the firm lead to more time I can spend paying more attention to myself and my family. This, in turn, gives me more energy to invest back in the firm.

And that means we're able to scale—and continue to scale across the country.

In fact, my health has given us such an edge that my firm now approaches the horizon where it has grown large enough and the culture is strong enough that we can start building into something far bigger than me.

CHAPTER 10

MOVING BEYOND YOU

TorkLaw was not the original name of my law firm. For the first three years, we were The Torkzadeh Law Firm. That seemed like the obvious choice. Looking around the city at other successful firms, that seemed to be the pattern they all followed. And if it worked for those guys, why wouldn't it work for me?

I don't mean to imply I put a whole lot of thought into this. To be honest, I never thought anything about it at all. When the firm didn't grow as quickly as I might have hoped, it never occurred to me to consider the name. The name was my own. I was proud of who I was and the firm I had founded. I never thought it should be any different.

I probably should have known better. You can imagine what it was like growing up with a name like Torkzadeh. The first day of school was always fun as I listened to teacher after teacher mispronouncing my name. But for some reason, I assumed that trouble wouldn't affect my business. Other firms used last names whether they were common or not. That was good enough to put my mind at ease.

I might have continued in this thinking if not for a book I picked up one weekend called *You Can't Teach Hungry* by John Morgan. The book made such an impression on me, I set up a meeting with John in Orlando a short time afterward. The plan was for me to spend the day with him, discuss business strategies over dinner, and fly back the next day. But that is not how the afternoon turned out.

It started off as planned. We went to lunch. John showed me around his office and told me a bit about how he ran his firm. He reviewed his philosophy on everything from running the country's largest personal injury law firm to his thoughts on life itself. After lunch, as we settled in back at his office, he asked me about my practice. Most likely, I told him far too much—how I'd started, where I was, where I wanted the firm to head, all the big cases I'd won.

"Great," he told me, as he picked up the phone on his desk and put it on speaker. "Let's get a clearer picture of how you're running things. What's the name of your firm?"

"The Torkzadeh Law Firm," I said.

He gave me a stony look and hung up the phone. "That's fucked up."

I couldn't believe what I was hearing. How was my name fucked up?

"Look," he explained, "Imagine someone calls 411 and wants to be connected to your firm. They've been in an accident, and they want to talk to you about representing them. How is that person going to pronounce your name? How is the operator going to spell it? How is anyone going to even remember your firm's name at that moment?"

I felt like I'd run into a brick wall. I actually felt a brief wave of panic overrun me. Have you ever had that feeling—a mix of embarrassment and regret—as you realize that you've committed the same mistake over and over again until someone shows you that there was a far easier way to do it? That was me in that moment.

But it wasn't going to be me any longer. Right after that discussion, I jumped on the next flight home. As soon as I landed, I went into the office, determined to find a name for my firm that people could remember.

Within days, The Torkzadeh Law Firm was a thing of the past. In its place was TorkLaw.

BREAKING THE COMMODITY MARKETING CYCLE

What I hadn't realized until that meeting with John Morgan was how important a name is to a business. Law firms often see themselves as outside the standard business rules, but we are really no different. Like most businesses in most industries, we're living in a world of commodity marketing, and a name is an important part of how we succeed within that system—and how we eventually overcome it.

Commodity marketing refers to the similarities between advertising and commodity trading. When you trade commodities, the idea is to buy at a certain price and sell at another to make a profit. If you stop selling, you stop making money. The same is true of advertising for most companies. You spend money to acquire clients. If you are advertising wisely, you make a profit on that transaction. But the moment you stop spending that advertising budget, the phone stops ringing and the clients go somewhere else.

This is the cause of much frustration for smaller firms. It is very hard to get those early clients when you can't afford to work the system like your bigger competition. We've already looked at some ways you can break into this cycle by growing a more authentic firm that connects through social media and develops good word-of-mouth through a strong, firm culture. But even using these strategies, at some point, you're going to have to spend on some advertising. That's just the nature of the modern market.

But it doesn't have to be this way. There's a way to break free of the commodity marketing system. To do that, you have to do what few firms have ever managed to achieve: build your firm into a brand.

PUTTING THE BRAND FIRST

During the Euro 2020 soccer tournament, Cristiano Ronaldo—one of the most famous and successful athletes in the history of sports—removed a bottle of Coca-Cola from the desk where he was taking questions and told the whole world to drink water instead. The next day, Coca-Cola's stock dropped. Within a month, it was back at its original value.

For most companies, having the biggest name in soccer tell

people to avoid your company would be a death sentence. But that's not the case for Coca-Cola because it is one of the few companies with a brand that can weather that bad press. The Coca-Cola brand is so strong, people will continue to drink it even if Ronaldo tells them not to.

This is the case with the best brands across industries. While Starbucks, like Coca-Cola, does have a large advertising budget, it doesn't take much to get the average coffee drinker to line up for one of their lattes every morning. Why? Because their brand is almost synonymous with coffee. The same is true of Amazon. Amazon's brand is so powerful that it's the first word anyone thinks of when they think of e-commerce. This kind of branding isn't just for mega-companies either. Companies like Got Junk or Roto Rooter have been able to dominate their industries by becoming the brand that people know beyond the advertising.

This is how you break the commodity marketing chain in the law industry as well. At this point, no firm has created a brand on this level. Even the biggest firms can't avoid investing huge amounts of money into advertising. The reason these firms can't escape commodity marketing is because all they've really achieved through that advertising is name recognition. As we've discussed before, the average client doesn't know whether that name represents good legal assistance or not. They just know the name. If the name stops appearing on billboards, people forget about it.

This is the biggest open opportunity in law, and if you run your firm right, you might be able to snatch it before the Wall Street investors get there first.

The key to taking the lead here will be the culture you've developed in your firm. If you look at the brands I've mentioned in this section, you'll notice one thing about them: they're all really good at what they do. A few years ago, McDonald's tried to cut into Starbucks' brand by promising better coffee. It didn't take—because everyone already knew that Starbucks had better coffee, and no amount of commercials was going to convince them otherwise. The same is true for Coca-Cola. No matter what Pepsi does, people will continue to drink Coke because they know it tastes better. Amazon is great at delivering products quickly and at a good price. They have no major competitors because no one can keep up with what they do.

That doesn't mean that advertising isn't important, but when you develop a brand around being the best at what you do, you can become *the* name in your space.

That's what your brand can stand for that no other firm does at the moment. Right now, a big firm is nothing but a name to people. Your firm can be a brand that stands for community, strong culture, and quality legal help. Once you establish that brand, all you have to do is continue to live up to those values.

TIME TO STEP BACK

So how do you build this brand? The answer may require a bit of tough medicine.

It's often said, if you want to make someone better, you tell them the truth, not what they want to hear. It's equally true that it's easier to take offense to tough advice than act on that advice. So I hope you will take it well when I tell you that the ultimate goal of your firm is for it to outgrow you.

Up to this point, I've advised you to put yourself—your vision, your principles, the causes you believe in—at the forefront of your firm. When you're a small firm, that's precisely what you need. You need to give that firm a personality and a culture that people in the office and clients outside of it can respond to. However, once you achieve that early growth, it's time to make another transition—one in which you step back from the front lines and let your firm run itself.

This is how the best companies develop their brand. Recently, Jeff Bezos stepped away from running day-to-day operations at Amazon. No one cared because everyone knew that he had built the company so well that it would continue to be equally well-run without him. Since Steve Jobs passed away, Apple has continued to gain market value because the culture he built outlasted him. The same has been true for Disney, which bears the name of its founder but which has only grown and improved since his passing because the vision he developed was bigger than him.

This is a key mistake firms make. Often, the limited branding they do is to put their founder's face on every piece of advertising and build the whole firm around that name and face. As we discussed in Chapter 1, though, that's a choice made out of ego, not smart business practice. Putting yourself upfront for all of your branding will only lead to problems down the line.

Once the firm grows large enough that you can no longer handle every case, you're setting yourself up to disappoint clients who sign up to work with you. And what happens when you want to step away or retire? If you're the face of the firm, that firm likely retires with you.

Instead of making your face and your name the brand, you need to allow the firm you've built upon your principles to stand on its own. And that takes another difficult step: letting go of the reins and trusting others to be leaders.

DELEGATION

At some point when scaling a firm, success can become your greatest enemy. The firm grows too big to handle, and if you fight against the need to entrust others with authority, it can break you. While things are small, you might be able to handle almost every task on your own. Once you grow, though, that becomes untenable. You can't answer the calls, order the medical records, run your marketing, and meet with every client and potential client.

Delegation is an absolutely critical part of growth. It's also critical to growing a firm beyond you. After all, the only way to allow the firm to take care of itself is to build up those within the firm who believe in the culture, share the vision, and know how to move forward on their own.

Knowing this, of course, doesn't make it any easier. But once you recognize the need for delegation, the process can be fairly simple—at least, if you've followed the advice in this book. The key to developing leaders within your organization is to hire the best people in the first place. Use the techniques we covered in Chapter 4 and bring in the best receptionists, the best intake specialists, and the best lawyers. Over time, you will notice individuals on each team that stand above the rest. They work a bit harder, they help their colleagues a bit more, and they display honesty and sound decision-making skills.

If you have the right people in place, this will always happen. All you have to do is pay attention and respond by giving these natural leaders more responsibility.

I've certainly found that at TorkLaw. Last year, I took a step I never thought I would. I elevated one of my lawyers to the position of Managing Attorney. She had been with the firm for years and always demonstrated strong leadership skills. That has proven one of the best decisions I've ever made for the firm. Not only have I delegated those responsibilities to a strong partner in the daily management of our firm (someone a lot smarter and better at that work than me), I've freed myself to fully take on my true role, that of the CEO.

A FIRM WALL STREET WOULD ENVY

When John Morgan told me that my firm's name was "fucked up," I could have taken offense. Deep down, though, I knew he was right. If I really wanted to realize my ambitions and build a hugely successful firm, I would need to do it with a different name.

These days, I'm thinking about changing the firm's name again. TorkLaw has served me well up until this point, but as I seek to build the sort of brand I've described in this chapter, I've realized that the story is still too much about me. I've begun the process of removing myself from that story because I truly believe the firm isn't just about me. It's about all the people who have come on board as employees or clients that believe in the values and vision that I've set out. At heart, we believe in helping anyone who has been injured under unjust circumstances—and the new iteration should reflect that belief instead of just connecting to my name.

I hope, someday, that our brand will break the commodity marketing cycle and TorkLaw—or whatever it is called by then—becomes a name associated with the type of law I believe in.

And I hope your firm is right there with mine, with a brand people believe in—and one any venture capitalist would dream of developing.

CONCLUSION

Back in 2012, I left a law firm I'd started five years earlier with a couple partners. That partnership was relatively prosperous, but I quickly found out there was much more to running a law firm than just being good at law. When I decided to venture out on my own, I had no one to reach out to for guidance about how to manage and grow my own law practice.

I'm sure many of the errors that I've recorded in this book—and many more that I've kept to myself—could have been avoided if I'd had a place where I could get some decent advice. Without help, it was all trial and error—and early on, it mostly came up error.

Wall Street investors are well aware of how independent law firms struggle to compete. Their plan is to exploit those difficulties and capture the entire industry. I hope this book has proven you can thrive without that kind of meddling. I also hope it helps you avoid many of my mistakes. Within these pages, you have the core features of any successful business. If you build your firm around that core, you can scale to compete with anyone.

What I can't provide in a book, however, is the mentorship I so desperately needed in those early days. Mentorship goes beyond advice on a page about implementing the right strategy. It's a personal bond that allows hands-on experience to guide the novice. It includes a sense of community and mutual understanding.

CEOs know the value of such relationships. That's why they have retreats and mastermind groups. It's why they often build strong social bonds with their peers outside the office.

A book can't give you these things, but if you are looking for a sense of community and mentorship to supplement the ideas in this book, I hope you'll consider looking into LawWorks. In 2018, my wife came up with the idea of providing solo and small law firms with a shared workspace and a built-in network of like-minded lawyers, experts and vendors that can help law firm owners build and scale their practices. LawWorks is a mastermind group designed specifically for lawyers who are looking to attain that cutting edge and create law firms of the future. It's a collaboration of lawyers with a wide range of experience all in one place, all of whom have access to one another in real time. A place where ideas are being discussed in your industry that are relevant to you.

These ideas go far beyond the advice in this book. This is a place you can go to find out how to harness that data you're beginning to gather to forecast and budget. It's a place to find those who know how to take these tools and plan for success no matter the obstacles ahead.

Looking back at that moment in 2012 when I made the leap to my own firm, I needed two resources: (1) basic guidelines on how to build a firm, and (2) a mentor to guide me through it all.

We've tried to create both for the next generation of lawyers. You have one in your hand. When you're ready to really take on those private-equity-backed megafirms, I hope you seek out the other at LawWorks.com.

ACKNOWLEDGMENTS

I would like to acknowledge the entire team at TorkLaw whom I have the privilege of working with everyday. I have been lucky enough to find team members who share my vision, believe in what we are doing, and work relentlessly and passionately to serve our clients.

I'd also like to thank all former team members who are no longer with TorkLaw for one reason or another—those tough but critical lessons I learned would never have been realized without you.

Special thanks to my entire publishing team and in particular to Seth Libby, who masterfully delivered countless hours of support, input, editing, and direction.

ABOUT THE AUTHOR

REZA TORKZADEH is the founder and CEO of TorkLaw, a people-focused personal injury law firm known for its innovative approach to law firm marketing, strategy, and growth. Reza's legal commentary has been featured in major national publications, and he's a frequently invited guest speaker on the topic of law firm management. Recognized in the top 5 percent of US attorneys by Thomson Reuters, Reza co-founded Law-Works in 2019, providing a shared workspace for lawyers to collaborate with colleagues, meet with clients, and grow their business with purpose.

Manufactured by Amazon.ca
Bolton, ON

33335301R00088